Delighting in God

A. W. Tozer

GRAPEVINE BOOKS

Published by
GRAPEVINE BOOKS

www.grapevinebooks.com
email: contact@grapevinebooks.com

Ordering Information:
Quantity sales: Special discounts are available on quantity purchases by corporations, associations, and others.
For details, reach out to the publisher.

First published by Grapevine Books, 2025

CONTENTS

Chapter 1
The Reality of Our Perception of God

O God, my heart pants for Thee as David's of old did. I long to know Thee in all the beauty of Thy self-revelation and in all of Thy perfection. The way into Thy heart may be difficult and treacherous, but I can bear the difficulties as long as I discover in them the fullness of Thy character and nature. Amen.

Whenever you find a man of God, you will also find an overwhelming passion for God that is almost beyond control. Not a curiosity about God, but a deep passion to experience God in all of His fullness. To know God is the one passion that drives a man into the very heart of God.

Our Bible abounds with Scriptures highlighting this very passion. Indulge me two of my favorites.

David passionately writes:

As the hart panteth after the water brooks, so panteth my soul after thee, O God. My soul thirsteth for God, for the living God: when shall I come and appear before God?

Psalm 42:1–2

As far as I am concerned, these verses sum up the heartbeat of the man David, whom God says was a "man after His own heart." David had many things in his life and was not a perfect man by any stretch of the imagination, yet I can safely say that his hunger for God was the thing that lifted him above everyone else and made him a man after God's own heart. David desired God at any cost, and reading his story, we discover what that cost was.

In the New Testament, we have a man by the name of Paul, who wrote:

That I may know him, and the power of his resurrection, and the fellowship of his sufferings, being made conformable unto his death; if by any means I might attain unto the resurrection of the dead.

Philippians 3:10–11

To know God was the overwhelming passion of the apostle Paul, and nothing else in his life mattered, neither life nor death. If we can understand a man's passion, we can begin to understand why he does or does not do certain things. This passion for God was not a casual thing. To truly know God as He desires and deserves to be known is not a casual thing, but a lifelong pursuit that ends only when we see Him face-to-face.

I have used the word passion, and I need to explain myself. Passion can be defined in two ways. First, there is the passion of the heart, and then there is the passion of the mind. Often these two are confused or used interchangeably. The difference is that the passion of the mind is swayed by outside influences, whereas the passion of the heart delves into the deep things of God. John the Beloved wrote, "Greater is he that is in you, than he that is in the world" (1 John 4:4). The passion of the heart has the greater power in a person's life—the power to transform into true godliness that which is acceptable to God and meets His requirements.

Unfortunately, most people waste their passion on temporal things, such as sports, entertainment, vacations, whereas the man or woman of God focuses on that which can truly satisfy the heart. The ways of passion undermine our integrity. Our passion for God should lift us above the elements of the world into the heavenly spheres, where God's praise is supreme.

I need to point out that there are three basic levels of knowing God.

First is the intellectual level. This is based entirely upon the evidence at hand. Later on, we will examine the idea that we can find God in nature. However, the intellectual level is where we begin. God gave us a mind and expects us to use it, especially in the area of knowing Him. Scientists have explored our world in great detail, and all you need to do is examine the evidence.

The intellectual level goes only so far. The next level is theological. This is organizing truth into what we call doctrine. Theology is great, and I believe in theology, which is simply the study of God. What could be more exciting than that?

All theology must be based upon the Word of God. Theology is not an end in itself, but rather points to the One who is greater than theology. When theology becomes an end in itself, it ceases to be a way into the knowledge of God.

What people need today is truth—truth organized in a way that allows us to understand what God is about. The primary problem with theology is that we have organized it according to man's prejudice. Theology should be the study of God, not our human interpretation of God. That is where we encounter problems. Is God a Calvinist or is He an Arminian? According to some theology, you must be one or the other.

We have the intellectual level and the theological level, but that is not enough. Let's move on to what I call the mystical level.

I always get in trouble when I use the word mystic. I know this word has been abused and misused, but I am not afraid of controversy. I think the word mystic covers quite nicely what I am trying to say.

Down through the years there have been great evangelical mystic writers. These writers were so in tune with God that all of them, without exception, suffered persecution at the hands of church authorities. Their concept of God was so pure and lofty and holy, the average person could not grasp it.

When I talk about the mystical level of knowing God, I am speaking of that which pierces the Cloud of Unknowing—the area that cannot be discerned by human knowledge and understanding, that rises above the intellect and even theology and goes into the area of experiencing the presence of God. Brother Lawrence put his thoughts about this in his book Practicing the Presence of God. This is what the mystical level is all about.

Yes, we need to have an intellectual level first. And yes, the theological level is necessary to keep within the confines of the revealed Word of God. But all of that leads us deeper and higher, if you please, into the very heart of God. If I am going to know God, I need to penetrate the manifest presence of God, where His character and nature have been revealed to me in never-ending wonder and amazement.

It is simply not enough to know about God. We must know God in increasing levels of intimacy that lift us above all reason and into adoration and praise and worship.

David was a man who understood this. He was a man after God's own heart. In spite of that, he was a man of like passions like the rest of us. He had feelings, problems, and difficulties. But in spite of all his human weaknesses, David had a passion for God that lifted him above all of his mistakes and weaknesses and brought him into the very heart of God himself. Oh, that we would be like David, a man after God's own heart.

Reading through David's Psalms always leaves me with a hunger and desire for God. It is not so much a man's journey that defines him, but his destination, and David's destination was God. David was not searching for a better life. He was searching for God. He was not looking for recognition, acclaim, or possessions. He was searching for God. Some of that stuff got in his way, but in the end, David's passion for God won out.

In the New Testament, we have the apostle Paul, who was a man of reason, a well-educated man in his day, and one of the top Pharisees in Israel. He was going places as far as his religious aspirations were concerned. He was deeply devoted to his career and had reasoned himself down the pathway to success.

In looking at Paul's life, none of his reasoning truly satiated his heart. An emptiness within spurred him on, only to be left empty once more. It was on the road to Damascus that Paul reached the end of reason and encountered God. He discovered God, and from that moment on, the passion of his heart can be summed up in the phrase "That I may know Him." No matter what else we know about Paul, if we know this, we begin to understand the real passion of his heart and why he did some of the things he did.

Paul's statement in Philippians 3:10–11 sums up the essence of his passion for God:

That I may know him, and the power of his resurrection, and the fellowship of his sufferings, being made conformable unto his death; if by any means I might attain unto the resurrection of the dead.

To know God was Paul's passion, and nothing else really mattered to him. Three things helped Paul focus on God (from the Scripture quoted above).

The first was "the power of his resurrection."

Becoming a Christian is not just nodding to a few truths and then saying, "I accept Jesus." It is infusing into your life the divine power, the same power that raised Jesus from the dead. This is the tremendous work of the Holy Spirit to bring you into the divine world of redemption.

The second was "the fellowship of his sufferings."

This was Paul's identification with the Christ who died on the cross and rose the third day. What Paul meant by this was that his Christianity was a result of his relationship with God. And Paul was willing to follow Him at all costs. This passion of Paul got him into a lot of trouble. I think I can safely say that Paul's attitude was that Christ's enemies were going to be his enemies and Christ's friends were going to be his friends.

Paul did not expect the world to treat him any better than people treated Christ. They crucified Christ, and they finally killed the apostle Paul. All of this was the result of his love for God that could not be satisfied with anything but God himself.

Paul's third focus was "being made conformable unto his death."

This was the key to the apostle Paul's ministry and the passion he had for God. When

Jesus died on the cross, it was for our sin. Paul speaks of putting "self" on the cross to free oneself from sin. It was his desire to bring his life into conformity with the death of Jesus Christ so that the resurrection power of Christ could usher him into worship and praise.

These two men, David in the Old Testament and Paul in the New Testament, started out from different points of view. They could not have been more different, and no two could have merged into one holy passion for God as they did. A person is known by the passion that drives him day after day through thick and thin.

What is needed today is passion, but more defined, a passion for God, a deep desire to know God as He desires to be known. What I see lacking today is this desire to know God on a personal basis. Other things crowd this relationship out until it is barely recognized in the church today.

In the evangelical church, we seem to have a great deal of passion for everything but God. We look around for activities that consume the resources of our lives. Instead of looking around at the world, we need to look up to the source of our redemption. We are so caught up with all the modern gadgets and methods that we have lost our passion for God.

I need a passion for God that penetrates that thick exterior known as the world, designed by the enemy to keep me away from God. Examining the conditions today, it is apparent our enemy has done a good job of establishing a wall between God and us that is all but impenetrable. Left to our own human resources, it would be impenetrable.

The important thing to keep in mind is that whatever keeps me away from God is my enemy, and only the power of God can overcome it. The trouble today is that we do not recognize the enemy and, in some cases, have even drawn him out to be a friend.

Isaac Watts puts this question before us: "Is this vile world a friend to grace, to help me on to God?" It is a rhetorical question, and the answer is a resounding no. Nothing in this world will in any way feed our passion for God. We must leave the world behind us and pursue on to know God in His arena. The closer I get to God, the further away from the world I become.

Coming into the presence of God is not something accomplished in human strength, as I pointed out, but only through the power of the Holy Spirit within me, enabling me to penetrate deep into the heart of God. The deeper into the heart of God I go, the more the enemy will oppose me, but the more God will draw me. The enemy may be strong, but his strength is limited, whereas God's grace has no limit. "Greater is he that is in you, than he that is in the world" (1 John 4:4).

I certainly am not against reason. I believe reason is a great asset in any pursuit in this world. It is essential that we are able to reason from point A to point B. Without reason the whole world would be in serious trouble. Scientists can uncover great mysteries by using reason. We live in a very rational world, despite many irrational people, and reason can be a great ally to us if we allow it. The problem is when we bring reason into the spiritual realm.

Reason by its very nature is limited and therefore cannot help us in our pursuit of the unlimited God. Reason may bring us to the door, but only faith can unlock the door that we may go into the presence of God. Faith is not unreasonable; it just operates above the reach of reason. Faith enables us to jump from one point on earth into the very heart of God.

The human heart has a thirst for God. God created us, and something in us relates to something in God. Until these two are brought together, which happens at salvation, there is restlessness within the human heart that can never be stilled.

This restlessness is seen in the world around us. The heart of the world is pulsating in a restless effort to discover the purpose of life, but it is always going in the wrong direction, away from God.

God created us with a passion for himself, and it was the fall of man in the garden of Eden that hijacked that passion and brought man down to the level we find him today. Only through redemption—accomplished by Christ dying on the cross and rising the third day—can we be brought back to that place of fellowship with God, which is the passion of every human being.

Paul's declaration "That I may know Him" is the war cry, if you please, of the redeemed soul pursuing God in the power of the Holy Spirit. The most natural thing following conversion is an insatiable desire to know God, which needs to be nourished with the deep things of God.

Peter declared this when he wrote, "But grow in grace, and in the knowledge of our Lord and Saviour Jesus Christ" (2 Peter 3:18). It is the passion of the Christian to grow, but the focus of our growth must be Christ. It is wonderful to know all the things around us, but to know Christ is the epitome of all knowledge. This is the passion of the Christian.

When I was younger, I sought to read and study everything I could get my hands on. I was a regular visitor at the local library and carried home armloads of books to read every week. I read biography, psychology, history, poetry, philosophy, and, yes, even theology. I could debate people on just about any subject that came up at the time, much to the chagrin of my friends around me.

As I got older and more mature in the things of God, I began to lose interest in those subjects, and I began to have a passion to simply know God. That is when everything changed. All the books I had read in the past faded in the light of knowing God. It has cost me dearly in my pursuit of God. However, as I look back, it is my pursuit of God that has brought me to where I am today. I desire to know God in all the beauty of the divine unfolding.

I have come to deeply appreciate the great hymns of the church. I realize that men who wanted to know God deeply wrote these hymns. As they searched for God, they put into poetry their findings. I am a richer man today from reading the poetry based on their findings about God.

Scarcely a day goes by but that, often on my knees, I sing one of the grand old hymns of the church. I certainly am not a candidate for the church choir, but I am a candidate for that heavenly choir that sings to God with such passion for the joy and pleasure of knowing Him.

O For A Thousand Tongues

O for a thousand tongues to sing

My great Redeemer's praise,
The glories of my God and King,
The triumphs of His grace!

My gracious Master and my God,
Assist me to proclaim,
To spread through all the earth abroad,
The honors of Thy name.

Jesus! The name that charms our fears,
That bids our sorrows cease;
'Tis music in the sinner's ears,
'Tis life, and health, and peace.

He breaks the power of canceled sin,
He sets the prisoner free;
His blood can make the foulest clean,
His blood availed for me.

Glory to God, and praise, and love
Be ever, ever given
By saints below and saints above,
The Church in earth and heaven.
Charles Wesley
(1707–1788)

Chapter 2

The Basis of Our Perception of God

O God, help me collect my thoughts and focus on Thee. I am so prone to wander and speculate, but, O Lord, lead me in the way of knowing Thee in such a way as to understand who I am and why I am here. Lead me on into Thy perfection in Jesus' name. May I be worthy to know Thee in all the fullness of Thy divine revelation. Amen.

A man would be a fool to try to attempt something beyond his capacity and ability. Anyone who would attempt to do what I have set before me would be a fool if he thought he could pull it off.

Even to talk about God requires a capacity beyond human ability. I know everyone talks about God, but in the context that I have set before us in this chapter, no one can truly talk about God in a way that is worthy of the God we are talking about. No man can preach about God worthily, no man can write about God worthily, unless that man knows God beyond his human ability.

I do not approach the subject as a scholar or a theologian. I believe in theology. I think nothing is more wonderful than theology, which is simply the study of God. All theology begins with God and ends with God, or it is not true biblical theology. Much that passes for theology today is simply the educated man trying to explain God through his own logic and reason. I assure you, there is plenty of logic and reason with God, but it does not stop there. If all we had was logic and reason, we would never penetrate that Cloud of Unknowing that keeps most people from truly knowing God.

We make a grave error when we approach such a subject as an expert. The church is full of experts these days, and they have only added to the confusion of our perception of God. The only way to approach the subject is as a worshiper. All the technical aspects of theology fall short of truly penetrating the manifest presence of God.

I am not giving a lecture on what I think about God. What I am doing is giving a witness, a testimony, if you please, of my journey into the heart of God. My witness is not for the head, but for the heart that has a burning passion to know God.

At risk of repetition, it was Saint Augustine who really understood this and wrote in his confessions, "Thou hast made us for Thyself, O Lord, and our heart is restless until it finds its rest in Thee." This man of God understood what many do not understand today. We were created for a purpose, and until that purpose is fulfilled, we are in a restless state. Nothing outside of us can bring the rest and peace we were created for and yearn for. The pleasures of the world fall far short of this. Not all the exterior aspects of the world can penetrate that sacred barrier of the soul reserved only for God. Our worship today is too emotional and fails to quiet our souls to fully experience the presence of God. It is my objective in this book to lead the hearts of believers toward God, in whom they will discover their purpose and find their rest.

In years gone by, men were quite unsure of themselves, but that day is far gone. Today we are very sure about ourselves, so sure about everything except the things that we should be sure about. We have majored in the minors and lost our true significance. More people back then had the mindset of Thomas Blacklock, who said, "Come, O my soul, in sacred lays [levels or stratums]."

Personally, I think it might be a good idea when we get together on Sunday mornings to make a point to call our souls "in sacred lays." Of course, today's congregations have no idea of what this truly looks like. This is something that needs to be explored today, and we need to follow Blacklock's prayer:

Come, O my soul, in sacred lays

Attempt thy great creator's praise:

But oh, what tongue can speak His fame?

What verse can reach the lofty theme?

When we begin to think about God, we are thinking about that which is beyond our ability to fully comprehend and beyond the limit of human intelligence. Very plainly put, if you can conceive it, it is not God.

I want to concentrate on the perfection of God, which includes all of those characteristics of His divine nature. Once you begin probing into the personality of God, there is no end in sight. It goes on and on as He delights to unfold himself before our worshiping hearts.

The more we know about God and the more we know Him intimately, the more we will begin to understand ourselves and that wondrous and mysterious connection we have with Him. God's attributes dictate the praise and worship acceptable to Him, and if it is not acceptable to Him in any regard, it is not suitable worship. We must evaluate our worship in light of the One we are worshiping. No one can do that and do it worthily, for who of us is capable of anything like that? The One we are worshiping dictates our worship.

In "Idylls of the King: The Passing of Arthur," Alfred, Lord Tennyson put it this way:

More things are wrought by prayer than this world dreams of.

Wherefore, let thy voice rise like a fountain for me night and day.

For what are men better than sheep or goats

That nourish a blind life within the brain,

If, knowing God, they lift not hands of prayer

Both for themselves and those who call them friend?

For so the whole round earth is every way

Bound by gold chains about the feet of God.

Quite frankly, I am dealing with the One you must believe in before you can deny Him: the One who is the Word, the One who enables us to speak concerning Him. On our own, we could produce only a caricature, and a poor one at that, and certainly not worthy of our worship. I refuse to worship anything of my own making.

I readily admit I am not qualified in myself to present such truths about God. The more I delve into the subject at hand, the more I realize how much I really do not know. Sometimes we can become so arrogant that we think we believe, but we are blinded to certain aspects of the truth. I certainly want my heart open to everything that God would reveal to me.

The thing that must really be understood is that our knowledge of God cannot be acquired simply through academic processes. What we really know about God is what He has faithfully revealed to us.

When Jesus rose from the dead and appeared to the disciples, they still could not believe. Belief is not based upon seeing, because if it were, they would have believed that Jesus was risen from the dead when they saw Him. It took a spiritual application of revelation that cannot be brought about by reason or logic. When their eyes were opened, which is only done through the work of the Holy Spirit, they were able to believe.

What the Holy Spirit does not reveal to us is not worth knowing.

It is my contention that everything we do in some way reflects our perception of God. It does not take long to understand a person when you begin to understand his or her perception of God. I believe it is critical that our perception of God be worthy of God and that it reflect the truth revealed to us about the God of the Word. Even those who do not believe in God make a god out of not believing in God. What is it that you really believe and think of when you hear the word God? Your perception of God determines everything about you. For this reason, our perception of God needs to be based on a solid foundation that will not let us down under any circumstance.

We need to really understand the history of man's progressive degeneration. Some believe man is on his way up. The evidence, however, does not support this idea at all. If man were on his way up, why is he still wrestling with the sins of his forefathers? Why is it that man has not solved his problems, but seems only to add to them?

The story begins in the garden of Eden. It was there that man began. Adam was created in the image of God, and upon his creation, God said about him, "It is good." There was no imperfection anywhere to be found in him. Such was also the case with Eve.

Some seem to say that a man's environment is what brings him down. A young boy growing up in the ghetto in the middle of the city does not have a chance. The other side of that is a young boy growing up in the suburbs, who has all the advantages of life, will turn out great. Evidence points in a different direction.

Adam and Eve were in the perfect environment. No sin was to be found anywhere in that wonderful garden—no imperfection of any kind, nothing that in any way would cause a man or a woman to turn their back on God. Enter Satan, man's enemy.

Up until this point, Adam and Eve had a good perception of God. He walked with them in the cool of the day. They had fellowship with Him that can only be imagined and envied from our side of the garden. They knew who God was. Then Satan threw in a seed of doubt, and the history of man took a downward spiral. Satan cast a bad reflection on God that caused Adam and Eve to question who God was and if He really had their best interests at heart. We all know where the story goes after that.

This progressive degeneration has been the theme of man's history since that time. Man's perception of God began to leave his mind, and he adopted the agenda of Satan: "I will be like the Most High." Since that time, man has tried to rise above God, only to fall into a downward spiral that eventually ends in the pit of hell.

The consequence of all this is that man lost his confidence in God. As a result, people do not have faith in God. We can look at the great men of faith. One that I like is George Mueller. The question people ask is "Why can't I have the faith of George Mueller?"

The only way you can have the faith of George Mueller is to have George Mueller's confidence in God. This is not something that comes from textbooks or lectures or any of the technical aspects of religion that are so prominent today. This confidence in God can come only when we begin to know God as He really is. It is my contention that only a true worshiper can know God.

Religion can teach you about God. Cold, textual theology can teach you about God. But neither can really bring you into the presence of God, where you begin to know God and have confidence in the God that you know. I contend that our faith in God comes naturally and automatically as we begin to know Him personally—not just know about God, but have a personal encounter with the living God, an encounter that is not boxed in by reason or logic. A true encounter with God lifts us above everything we can know, and we begin to pierce that Cloud of Unknowing and come into the presence of God.

Faith is not something we struggle to build. Rather, faith is knowing God, believing in God and what He says about himself, resulting in confidence in God and His character. "Faith cometh by hearing, and hearing by the word of God" (Romans 10:17).

If we have to struggle to try to drum up faith, it will be a pseudo-faith and nothing that will enhance our walk with God. Our confidence in God will plummet, and we will begin looking for a replacement. I am so afraid that the Christian church today has found its replacement in entertainment and social activities.

But my task is to give a report on the character of God, or as I like to state it, the perfection of God. I want to tell you what God is like, and when I am telling you what God is like, if you read and listen with an open mind, you will find faith spring up automatically. It takes the restored knowledge of God to bring forth our faith. I do not believe there was ever a time in the history of the church when we needed this more than we need it today.

Someone once complimented me by telling me they thought I was a good preacher and they got a great deal out of my sermons. When I was younger, I might have agreed, but I have listened to recordings of some of my sermons and they sound awful, to tell you the truth. I do not claim to be a good preacher. However, I do preach about good things, and that is what makes a vast difference between a good preacher and preaching about something good. I am preaching about something good when I am preaching about God; I am now writing about that which is good and above everything else we could even think about.

This is the core and center and source of all theology and all doctrine and all truth, all life and all matter and all mind, all spirit and all soul. This is the great need of the hour because the situation, as I see it in churches today, is very serious. It is not how well we say it, but rather how well we believe it.

Knowing God is to understand our reason for existence—our purpose in life. Life is so short that many people waste it trying to find themselves—outside of God. This knowledge transcends reason and comes to us only by way of divine revelation and illumination. Keep in mind, ideas of God not rooted in revealed truth give way to human speculation and certain untruths about God, and disqualify any worship we might try to give to God.

My prayer for you is that this book will stir up in you a holy passion to know God. The sooner this book is unnecessary, the sooner you will begin to discover your relationship with God, and when that takes place, your soul will begin to sing the song of worship and praise and adoration.

Come, O My Soul, In Sacred Lays

Come, O my soul, in sacred lays
Attempt thy great creator's praise:
But oh, what tongue can speak His fame?
What verse can reach the lofty theme?
What verse can reach the lofty theme?

Enthroned amid the radiant spheres,
He glory like a garment wears;
To form a robe of light divine,
Ten thousand suns around Him shine,
Ten thousand suns around Him shine.

In all our Maker's grand designs,
Almighty power, with wisdom, shines;
His works, through all this wondrous frame,
Declare the glory of His name,
Declare the glory of His name.

Raised on devotion's lofty wing,
Do thou, my soul, His glories sing;
And let His praise employ thy tongue
Till listening worlds shall join the song,

Till listening worlds shall join the song.

Thomas Blacklock

(1721–1791)

Chapter 3
Our Perception of God and the Church

O God, my heart is empty because I can find nothing to adequately fill it. I need Thee to fill me with all the fullness of Thy perfection. Lead me, O God, in the path of righteousness that I might discover Thee and the truth of Thy character and nature. Amen.

Anyone who has been even a casual observer of the evangelical Christian church over the last generation or two would agree when I say there has been significant growth, which has been effected by the overall perception of God in our midst. I am often accused of being negative, and I struggle with it, but I also like to put forth the true picture. Some wonderful advancement in the Christian church has been a blessing, of which I am grateful to God.

I want to be faithful in acknowledging the success of the church in doing what God has called her to do. I want to celebrate the victories the church has won during the last generation or two. Nothing gives me more pleasure than to see God's blessing resting upon His church.

It all boils down to what a man believes about God. His perception of God becomes the foundation upon which he builds his whole life, and out of that flows the spirit of worship, and out of his worship flow service and ministry.

I need to lay down something rather important—that is, the church's witness, if it is going to be valid, has to be related to its times. A sermon to be preached, a book to be published—if they are to mean anything—have to relate to the day in which they are given. Nothing of any value has ever come out of a vacuum. Therefore, what I have to say will be in the context of the current religious situation. If we are going to know anything about a spiritual situation, we need to take a very close and honest look at the whole situation at hand.

I want to look at the evangelical situation for the moment. I am not interested in anything but the situation of the evangelical church, that is, I have nothing to say about liberal or modernistic churches. If we're going to know where we are and where we are going, we need to know how we got here and what kind of spiritual situation we are in. We are going to have to appraise ourselves in light of our gains and our losses.

Allow me to outline some of the gains I see in the evangelical church of today.

The Religious Spirit

The first I will mention is the fact that in the last generation there has been an amazing resurgence of the religious spirit. Religion has become quite popular in our time, and it is always easier to evangelize when you are in friendly territory. Everybody seems to know something about Christianity and God and Christ and the gospel. It gives us a platform to do our work.

Many have been greatly fooled by this. They believe because there is more religion in the world the world is better. We forget that there is simply a mighty resurgence of the religious spirit, and it has affected every religion in the whole wide world: Shintoism, Buddhism, Islam, and all the various "isms" and fringe cults, virtually all the religions of the world. In this upsurge of the religious spirit, evangelical Christianity has also felt a resurgence of religious feeling and has made quite a bit of gain.

I can remember back when my hair was black—and I had some—you had to be a doubter or an agnostic or an outright unbeliever to be respectable intellectually. Now we have witnessed quite a change, for you can believe in God and still not blush, and keep your respectability.

Churches

One thing we need to rejoice in is the growth of the evangelical church in our generation. Gospel churches are starting and growing and maintaining a significant presence in our culture. This can only be a good thing.

I am not sure if our Bible colleges and seminaries are keeping up with the need for pastors, ministers, and workers in these congregations. All of this represents a wonderful accomplishment, and I would be the last person to criticize the resurgence of evangelicalism in our country today. I celebrate progress if it is truly progress and pray for it to increase until Jesus comes.

Christian Education

Never before in the history of the church have we had more institutions to educate and train Christian workers than we do today. It is important that we have such institutions.

It seems that hardly a day goes by but somebody is starting some new Christian college, seminary, or Bible institute. By this, we have the means by which we can train people for the work of the ministry and fill these growing churches. I do not think the church has ever had a better trained group of ministers and workers to guide the church than it does today. I want to go on record as saying that I fully believe in Christian education. I believe a person should get as much education as they possibly can. I am never against that

Christian Publishing

Today more books are being published than ever since the invention of the printing press by Johannes Gutenberg in 1440. I am most grateful for the invention of the printing press and its development down through the years, making it possible for gospel literature to be published. We are blessed with an increasing flood of periodicals and tracts, along with an increase and improvement in the methods of communication like never before.

Stop and think some time of the busy, nonstop presses that are pouring out these days tons of religious literature. Everything that you could imagine, we have; you name it, and somebody is publishing it or will publish it. The evangelical church is certainly getting its message out.

Communications

Communications is an area that is rather fascinating. During my lifetime, communications has literally exploded. It seems that there are no limits to the development of communications technology.

As churches take advantage of modern technology and communications, they are able to spread the gospel throughout the world. In thinking about that, I wonder if there is a place anywhere in the world that cannot be touched with the gospel message. Is there a limitation to our communication of the gospel in our generation? And along with communications comes transportation. We are able to get to places quicker than ever before. Out on the mission field in years past, it took missionaries weeks to get from one place to a village they wanted to evangelize. Today, with the advancement of communications and transportation, they can get to that place in a matter of hours.

Christian Missions

There are also more missions and missionary activities and world evangelism than ever before. It would be impossible for anyone to count how many organizations there are along this line, and they are growing each year. We have more missions now than we know what to do with, and evangelism is riding very high. It is popular and gaining great momentum in our culture. The funding for these mission endeavors is growing every year. Evangelicals are contributing financially to the work of the ministry and missions.

We have evangelistic organizations to reach everyone: organizations for the evangelization of children, young people, housewives, Native Americans, railroad men, artists, and just about anybody. You name it, and I probably can find an organization that is busy evangelizing that particular group of people. No one has an excuse for not hearing the gospel today.

I would challenge you to find a group anywhere in the world, or a language anywhere in the world, to which somebody is not taking the gospel. We have so fine-tuned the gospel message to reach every tribe and tongue and nation. This, of course, is the focus of the Great Commission.

We are successful in evangelizing people, which is why we have greater numbers and why we have to have more committees and more schools. Much good is coming out of this.

I must say that I am all in favor of using the latest means and methods as long as they do not in any way compromise the message. Whatever makes the message secondary should be eliminated. We are obligated to God to get the message out to all the world by any and all means at our disposal. Our sacred obligation is to make sure the message is delivered unaltered, uncompromised, or "improved upon."

All of this, as I said, is much in our favor, and I want to acknowledge as much as I can. I pray daily for those who are involved in reaching the unsaved for Christ. This is a priority in our evangelical ministry.

When we talk about gains, we need to have a time of evaluation. A businessman learns at the end of the year how his business stands by balancing his losses against his gains. If he has more gains than losses, he has had a successful year, and he stands to increase his business the following year. If, however, he experiences too many losses, he probably will be out of business by the next year. Gains and losses need to be under control and evaluated. This is the rule of business.

The church, however, is not a business. Let me be clear on that point. But just as everything needs to be evaluated, the good and the bad duly noted, so in the church we need to have periodic evaluations as well. If we are going in the right direction, then we need to continue to go in the right direction and thank God for His leading. If there are some problems and difficulties, then corrections need to be made to bring us back to where we need to be.

As an editor, I know a manuscript needs to be reworked quite a few times before it is publishable. A good editor needs to edit out all unnecessary words and phrases so that the piece can be strengthened. I believe the same needs to be done in the church. We need to look at what we are doing and evaluate those things that are unnecessary and that are weighing down the church. I believe we need some very serious editing in the evangelical church today.

We need to evaluate where we are and what we are doing, by some measure. What is that measure? How do we know if what we are doing is correct or not?

Moses was instructed to make sure that the tabernacle was "according to the pattern shewed to thee in the mount" (Hebrews 8:5). Moses did not have the authority to improve upon God's design. The pattern God gave Moses was not a suggestion, and then Moses could take artistic license, as we say. The tabernacle, in order to be approved by God, had to be according to the pattern shown to Moses.

The pattern was a revelation to Moses, and Moses was faithful to that pattern.

This is where we need to get back to in the church. We need to understand what the pattern is, and that God has given us a pattern. Everything we do must be in complete harmony with that pattern. To improve upon the pattern, to compromise the pattern, is to incur God's displeasure.

I am sure Moses could have assembled a group of talented, artistic people to examine the pattern and then develop something far more elaborate than what God had in mind. I wonder if that is what is happening today? I wonder if we are not going beyond the pattern God has given us in the New Testament church?

In our evaluating the great advances and victories in the Christian church, we need to compare it to the New Testament pattern. This involves some painstaking evaluation and going back to the original drawings.

The Church's One Foundation

The Church's one foundation

Is Jesus Christ her Lord,

She is His new creation

By water and the Word.

From heaven he came and sought her

To be His holy bride;

With His own blood he bought her

And for her life He died.

'Mid toil and tribulation,

And tumult of her war,

She waits the consummation
Of peace forevermore;
Still, with the vision glorious,
Her longing eyes are blest,
And the great Church victorious
Shall be the Church at rest.

Yet she on earth hath union
With God the Three in One,
And mystic sweet communion
With those whose rest is won.
With all her sons and daughters
Who, by the Master's hand
Led through the deathly waters,
Repose in Eden land.

O happy ones and holy!
Lord, give us grace that we
Like them, the meek and lowly,
On high may dwell with Thee:
There, past the border mountains,
Where in sweet vales the Bride
With Thee by living fountains
Forever shall abide!
Samuel J. Stone
(1839–1900)

Chapter 4
A Defective Perception of God

Our Father in heaven, liberate me from myself and make me aware of the gulf between Thee and me. Lead me down the path to right that which is wrong and lead me into the way of reformation. I need a great move in my heart of the blessed Holy Spirit. Restore the fragrance of Thy presence. Amen.

In spite of the amazing advances that we have seen in the church, one great overwhelming loss troubles me greatly. The gains are wonderful, but they do not offset the one devastating loss, and that is the loss of a proper perception of God.

If we are going to offset the losses in the evangelical church over the last generation, something drastic needs to take place. I am hesitant to use the word revival because it is used rather carelessly. Perhaps the word reformation is more in order here. The church of Jesus Christ today needs a drastic reformation to bring it in line with its original design laid out for us in the Scriptures.

Everything seems to be a revival. I saw a sign that said, "Revival Tonight at 7 p.m." What I want to know is, how do they know a revival is going to take place at that particular time?

Perhaps it is because we have changed the meaning of the word revival, and we need to upgrade our vocabulary. Revival is not just getting together for some religious hootenanny. If you study the history of revival, you will come away with a deep sense of reverence for this concept.

In history, revival was indeed a move of God among His people to bring them back. It seems strange to me that the average gospel church wants to go forward, but forward in the wrong direction. When revival takes place, God brings us back, back to where we left God, where we left our first love. That is the key element.

Revival is to breathe new life, but not just any life; it is the breath of God upon an assembly of believers. Revival can take place only among God's people and can be done only by the Holy Spirit. One of the churches in Revelation was deemed lukewarm. They were neither cold nor hot. They started out right, had good intentions, were on a good path, but somewhere along the way, their love for God went flat.

When the great Welsh revival came to the little country of Wales in 1904 under the leadership of Evan Roberts, God had something to work on. This is a problem today. There is not much for the Holy Spirit to work on when it comes to a move of God in our midst. Back then, the Holy Spirit had something to work on. At times, the pastor on a Sunday morning never preached a sermon because God was working in such a way that he never got around to it. The Holy Spirit was moving in such a wondrous, overwhelming way that nobody could interject themselves. All they could do was to sit in the awesome silence of God's presence.

They sang hymns from The Psalter, the Holy Spirit moved in the congregation, and nobody could preach. As a result of this spiritual discipline, the people's perception of God was high and lofty, enabling the people who truly believed in God. My contention is that we have lost this lofty perception of God, and the church today, the evangelical church, is thin, anemic, frivolous, worldly, and cheap. I do not know how else to describe it.

In those revival services of days gone by, the people lost all track of time and were conscious only of the presence of God at work in their lives. Now the only thing people are conscious of in our churches is a spirit of entertainment and fun and frivolity, and "How soon will this be over so I can get back to the real world?"

One of my biggest concerns is in the area of preaching. We no longer have the kind of preaching that stirred congregations of the past. I am not one to be constantly looking back, but I think we can look back and see how far we have come. I do not believe we can go back. However, I think we need to understand that the preaching from the times of the early apostles up through men like John Wesley and then Charles Finney is quite different from today.

I realize the times have changed and the great temptation is to try to keep up with the times, whatever that may mean. The preaching that has stirred the church the most has been hard preaching of the Word of God, irrespective of the feelings or trends in the culture. This preaching was not to entertain, but rather to stir the hearts in worship of God. The focus of the preaching was God.

Read the famous sermon by Jonathan Edwards "Sinners in the Hands of an Angry God." The sermon so stirred New England that it gave birth to what was later called the Great Awakening. Moreover, that sermon and sermons like it brought congregations to a sense of holy fear and dread of God. We do not fear God anymore. We do not dread Him anymore. He is our buddy and wants only to help us be the best kind of people we can possibly be.

Today's preaching focuses on entertaining. If we can entertain the people, we can keep them. If we cannot keep the people, the church cannot grow. Therefore, whatever gets the people in and keeps them, that is what preachers are committed to. And that one word, entertainment, is in my mind a blasphemous word in the Christian culture.

The kind of preaching that stirred the church in the past is the preaching we need in the church today.

I almost hate to mention reading material. I think of the great classics that have blessed the Christian church for centuries and how God has used that literature. Today the literature—if you want to call it that—has been so dumbed down so as to not stir up anybody to holy passion. Today's literature is cheap junk that I believe should be shoveled out and thrown where it belongs.

From a rather personal perspective, I would like to be the pope for about twenty-four hours, just long enough to get a bull going—a papal bull. My first papal bull would read something like this: "I hereby prescribe all religious junk published in the last year to be thrown out." Just as soon as they got rid of it all, I would give back the pope position and retire.

Then listen to the songs being sung in so many places. Ah, the roster of the sweet singers. There is Isaac Watts, the little man that nobody would marry because he was so homely, but he wrote hymns, and what hymns he did write. Meditating on an Isaac Watts hymn will take you further into the presence of God than any song sung today.

Also, there was Nicolaus Zinzendorf, an accountant and wealthy businessman, who was marvelously converted in the Moravian church. He became the leader in the church, and under his ministry came a great revival. Some of his hymns were "Jesus, the Lord, Our Righteousness"; "O Come, Thou Stricken Lamb of God"; "Jesus, Thy Blood and Righteousness"; and "Jesus, Still Lead On." Ah, and what hymns.

Then there were men like Charles Wesley, Isaac Newton, William Cowper ("There Is a Fountain Filled with Blood"), James Montgomery, Bernard of Cluny, and Bernard of Clairvaux. Then there was Paul Gerhardt, Tersteegen, Kelly, Anderson, and Toplady. The list goes on and on of the sweet singers of God.

Some of the junk sung today should not be tolerated in our churches. The reason it is tolerated is that our church leaders do not know any better. Sad, but true, we have the blind leading the blind today. Our singing is too frivolous and meaningless and does not give God His rightful due. This tragic and frightening decline in the spiritual state of the church has come about as a result of our forgetting what kind of God our God is. Unless we get to know what God is like, unless we know God, we will accept all the superficial nonsense that passes for Christianity today. Our perception of God determines our perception of worship.

What is it that the church has lost?

When I say lost, please do not think everybody has lost it, because God always has His seven thousand who have not kissed Baal or bowed down to his image.

If we are going to make any kind of progress, we need to understand what we have really lost.

At the very foundation of our loss today is what I call the "vision of the majesty on high."

Today we are democratic in distinction from autocratic; we slap our kings and leaders on the back and call them "Bud" these days. The concept of majesty is gone from the world, and in particular, it is gone from the church.

Majesty is a word nobody uses today. But we just do not know what the word means anymore. We have become the generation of the common man and have managed to beat down every uncommon man until he is a common man. And if anybody by sheer hard study, prayer, and work sticks up his head a little above the rest, we beat him down and call him "Bob" just to prove to him that we are somebody and he is nobody. We have lost the concept of majesty.

I mourn this loss of majesty that I see permeating the church. I believe it would do every Christian good to read through the book of Ezekiel, preferably on their knees. In this book of that old prophet, there is that terrible, frightful, awful passage where the Shekinah, the shining presence of God, flies out from between the wings of the cherubim and goes to the altar. From that altar it rises and goes to the door and, with the sound of whirring wings, to the outer courts and to the mountain, and finally into glory.

The Shekinah glory that followed Israel disappeared. Perhaps God could take it no longer, so He pulled out His majesty and the Shekinah went with Him. I wonder in how many churches this would be true. I wonder how many churches really have experienced the overwhelming majesty of God's presence in their worship. I feel too many are experiencing the silence of God. God has no welcoming invitation into the worship services today. Everything is programmed. Everything is developed from the mindset of mankind to please mankind. Once again, we need to see the terrible, majestic, awesome presence of God, the holy Shekinah, in our worship times today.

One hour in the presence of the majesty of God is worth more to you now and in eternity than all the preachers, including me, who have ever stood up to open their Bibles.

To study the history of the Christian church down through the ages, it is easy to see that she lived on the character of God alone. Unlike religions that have come and gone throughout the centuries, Christianity surpasses them all, especially in this one area: magnifying the character of God.

Religion is all about work and gaining God's approval. History shows us that this is impossible.

Christianity is all about worshiping God, celebrating and delighting in the amazing character of God. No other religion has risen as high as Christianity in its relationship to God. Everything about Christianity is focused on God. The church has preached God, prayed to God, declared God among the nations, honored God, and elevated God in every generation. When the church is acting like the church, God is being exalted among the nations.

For some reason, the church has grown bored with this. It is hard to explain why, but we have succumbed to the lowly concept of God expressed in religion. Where once we had a high and lofty perception of God, we have allowed, for some reason, the world to redefine our God for us. Instead of taking our God to the world, the world is bringing a god to us that is acceptable to them.

The world wants a pal, a partner, and even, as someone has said, "The man upstairs who likes me."

Even Hollywood has injected itself into this act. An actress from California happened to be in New York City, crawling around among the saloons, blowing smoke and soaking up liquor. She got into a religious conversation with somebody who happened to ask if she was a religious person.

"Yes," she said, "I am a religious woman. The fact is I know God. Do you know God?"

The man looked at her, smiled, and said he did not know God.

"Well," she said, "you better get to know God. You will find if you get to know Him, He is a living doll."

So, we have God as a "living doll."

No religion in the world that I know of would treat its God the way we Christians treat our God. We have the true God, yet we do not treat Him with the respect and dignity that the heathen treat their gods.

I must confess there are times when I am tempted to turn my back on a lot that passes for Christianity in our day. In my opinion, it is not Christianity, and something needs to be done to rattle the cage to get people to see how despicable their concept of Christianity has become.

We have taken all the carnal expressions of the world and put them on God. Prayer is "going into a huddle" with God. I have heard this expression, and I only can conclude that it comes from people who do not have a proper perception of God. To know God and then disrespect Him is the epitome of hypocrisy. For many people, prayer is simply a way to convince God to give you something you want. That kind of prayer never gets above the ceiling.

For many today, God is only the top celebrity—that is all. If God were to come to earth now, they would sign Him up for some television show immediately. They would have a story called This Is Your Life, and then tell God how He got the way He is. God is only the top celebrity, and in the meantime, Christianity has lost its dignity when it comes to the things of God.

I do not believe we need more religion; we need a better kind of religion. My great burden these days and for many years has not been for an extension of the kind of religion we have now. It has to be an improvement of the kind we have and then an extension of that. The one great loss we have suffered in the evangelical world, the one great overwhelming, calamitous loss that has been the cause of all these other losses is one: a loss of God. The most high God, maker of heaven and earth—that awesome God before whom our fathers fell—that God has left us, and in His place has come that God of the half-saved, who want to get chummy with God and treat Him like the chairman of some committee.

Religious Fear

We also have lost from our gospel Christianity—almost altogether—what used to be called "religious fear." We have practically no religious fear in our time, and along with our loss of religious fear has come a corresponding flippancy and familiarity toward God that our fathers never knew.

The God of our fathers has been replaced by many other gods who are in no way able to actually replace our God. The problem with that is this god is not the God of Abraham, Isaac, and Jacob, but a god of thought—a god of our empty heads—and the result is that he can never surprise anybody, he can never transcend anything, he can never beat anybody down, he can never crush anybody, he can never lift up anybody. He is just a nice, comfortable god to have around, halfway between Plato and John Wesley.

The Art of Worship

With the loss of the concept of majesty comes the loss of the art of worship. We no longer worship. I am not sure what we do, but it does not contain the reverence and the awesome wonder about God that our forefathers cherished. The only worship that is acceptable is that which is in complete harmony with the holy character and nature of God. After all, it is God whom we are worshiping, not ourselves.

The Loss of Our Inwardness

If Christianity is anything, it is an inward religion. Jesus said that we are to worship in spirit and in truth. We have such a tough outer shell that it is almost impossible for us to have those inward moments basking in the presence of God.

The Loss of an Awareness of the Invisible and the Eternal

The world is too much with us, and we have it with us all the time and all around us so that the invisible and the eternal seem to be quite forgotten. At least we are not aware of it. We are only briefly aware of it when someone dies. We are people of the "now generation."

The Loss of the Consciousness of the Divine Presence

Our churches today have lost consciousness of God's divine presence because we have lost the perception of deity that makes it possible. Come to church on Sunday and you may feel a sense of God and His presence, but when you leave, you leave that behind. Never should we leave the sense of God behind us. However, we have lost awe, wonder, holy fear, and spiritual delight. We have lost the high and lofty perception of God that God honors.

If we have lost that which is inward and gained only that which is outward, I wonder if we have gained anything at all. I wonder if we might not be in a bad state, spiritually speaking. I believe that we are and desperately need a fresh manifestation of God's power.

I Sing the Mighty Power of God

I sing the mighty pow'r of God,

That made the mountains rise,

That spread the flowing seas abroad,

And built the lofty skies.

I sing the wisdom that ordained

The sun to rule the day;

The moon shines full at His command,

And all the stars obey.

I sing the goodness of the Lord,

Who filled the earth with food,

Who formed the creatures through the Word,

And then pronounced them good.

Lord, how Thy wonders are displayed,

Where'er I turn my eye,

If I survey the ground I tread,

Or gaze upon the sky.

There's not a plant or flow'r below,

But makes Thy glories known,

And clouds arise, and tempests blow,
By order from Thy throne;
While all that borrows life from Thee
Is ever in Thy care;
And everywhere that we can be,
Thou, God, art present there.

Isaac Watts
(1664–1748)

Chapter 5
Restoring Our Perception of God

Our hearts, O God, ache as we think of how far we have fallen from Thy glory. We pray Thou wilt restore to us once again the glory of who Thou art. Forgive us for falling so far short of the glory that has established Thy name. Forgive us for allowing elements of the world to crush the glory that only belongs to Thee. Restore us to that place where once again we delight in Thee. Amen.

My major concern is not to focus on the negative aspects of the church today. Certainly, those things need to be pointed out with clarity, and we need to see the dire situation the church is in today. We dare not gloss over the spiritual losses if we are going to be honest and true to the Word of God.

God's Word does not allow ignoring the spiritual situation before us. We have an obligation to point out what is wrong and then, as John the Baptist did, point to the Lamb of God that taketh away the sin of the world. "Therefore to him that knoweth to do good, and doeth it not, to him it is sin" (James 4:17).

Of what value would a doctor be if when examining his patient he ignored some symptoms detrimental to his patient's health? Because of his medical profession, he bears an obligation and responsibility to deal with the medical well-being of his patient. If he sees something wrong, he has an obligation to point it out and then recommend or prescribe a cure.

That, then, is the purpose of this book: to be faithful to point out that the evangelical church today has some serious spiritual problems, the primary one being a loss of the perception of God that has been its hallmark since its inception.

I do not believe we can ever regain our lost perception of God until we are brought to consider once again the perfection of God. We must restore the biblical concept of God's perfection made so clear to us. I do not believe we can know everything about God. God is so vast that there is actually no way we can comprehend in its entirety the glory of our God. What we can do is fully comprehend those things He has revealed to us by the Holy Spirit through the Word of God.

The awesomeness and beauty and perfection of our God need to be the focus in our evangelical churches today. All efforts need to be directed here. I know the temptation is to correlate the church with the world in our misguided attempt to reach the world. But you cannot reach the world by becoming like the world. The only way to reach the world is to become something altogether other than the world. That is what we have in Christianity.

Once again we need to preach sermons in this regard. Songs need to be written and sung on this theme. We need once again to cultivate the inwardness of our Christianity and set that theme on fire in our generation. Oh, for the fire of the Holy Spirit on our congregations once again, but not the artificial fire of human ingenuity. Sometimes we have the desire to see something happen, and we do everything within our human ability to make it happen. This is not the source of the fire needed in our churches today.

If we are to restore a holy perception of God, we need to do it in such a way that it honors

God's character and nature. We need to push and push in this direction until men and women are caught in this holy flame of desire for God.

Personally, I have a passion to turn people away from the externals of religion and help them experience the marvelous internals of our Christianity that God has established for us. I know the difficulty of this task. My prayer is that God will raise up men and women who will be so aflame with the fire from the altar that nobody can put out the flame. Today's church needs once again to see the glory of God.

I know that people today are interested in sermons on how to be better people and get along in the world and be prosperous. Many preachers accommodate this thirst for the superficial, and rarely do you hear anyone simply preaching about God. There are a few out there who are interested in this theme, but not enough preachers who are so committed to it as to stir up a movement in our generation in this direction. I pray that God would set the hearts of many preachers on fire for this one thing. Let us forget all the other superficial stuff and press on to the perfection of our God and manifest Him in this generation.

I would like to see in the church today a restored perception of God in His majestic holiness.

Once again, we need to show God in His glory as it was in the days of Moses. It was a bold Moses who approached God:

And he said, I beseech thee, show me thy glory. And he said, I will make all my goodness pass before thee, and I will proclaim the name of the LORD before thee; and will be gracious to whom I will be gracious, and will show mercy on whom I will show mercy. And he said, Thou canst not see my face: for there shall no man see me, and live. And the LORD said, Behold, there is a place by me, and thou shalt stand upon a rock: And it shall come to pass, while my glory passeth by, that I will put thee in a clift of the rock, and will cover thee with my hand while I pass by: And I will take away mine hand, and thou shalt see my back parts: but my face shall not be seen.

Exodus 33:18–23

I believe we need this kind of boldness today if we are ever going to have restored to us the awesomeness of the God we serve and worship. Where are those men and women who will step out on a limb, so to speak, and demand to see God's face, those who will not give up until they encounter God in personal experience?

It will cost us to do this, and many are not willing to pay the price. As God is my witness, this is my prayer, not only for me, but also for all those who would follow in His train. We need to get to the mount of holiness and encounter God in the majesty of His perfection. And as Moses was not the same when he encountered God, neither will we be the same when we come face-to-face with God.

If we are to recapture our perception of God, we need to comprehend His perfection. We need to pierce the Cloud of Unknowing and enter into the perfection of our God.

I have used the word perfection, and I need to define what I mean by this. Consult Webster's dictionary and perfection means "the highest possible degree of excellence." Perfection means that which lacks nothing it should have and has nothing it should not have. It is fullness, completeness, not lacking in anything, and not having anything it should not have.

That is what I mean when I use the word perfection.

The difficulty is that we define perfection from our perspective. Consequently, it does not give us a good view of God when we think of the perfection of God. We think of perfection in a relative sort of way. If you have two things and one is better than the other, we assume the better one is to be the perfect one. In this regard, perfection means it is better than something else. And we use this all the time from a human perspective.

In music, for example, one singer is better than another, so we assume a state of perfection for the better singer. But you can always find another singer who sings better. Then their perfection slides into second place. Perfection cannot go up or down when we think about God.

Parents believe that their baby is perfect. In their eyes she is. But how can everybody's baby be perfect? There is a relative aspect when we use the word perfection. Our perfection is better, in our own eyes, than someone or something else.

In this regard, our use of perfection is focused on created things. Even singers whom we consider perfect, in a few years, may lose some of the perfect quality of their singing. As they get older, they lose some of that quality.

The baby who was born absolutely perfect will grow up to be a rather imperfect adult. Our idea of perfection has a "now" perspective to it.

When we come to God and the use of perfection with God, this does not stand. What applies to a creature can never apply to the Creator. A creature has ascending and descending levels of perfection. But when we come to the Creator, there are no ascending and descending levels of perfection. What God is at any one moment is what God is all the time.

As the Uncreated One, God has no degrees. With us, degrees are what identify us. One day we are happy. The next day we are down in the dumps and do not know what we are going to do next. One day we have joy. The next day we have sadness. We are up and down and up and down all the time.

When we come to God, we cannot compare God with anything or anyone else. There are two categories: the Creator and the creation. What is true in one category is not true in the other. "To whom then will ye liken me, or shall I be equal? saith the Holy One" (Isaiah 40:25). What God is saying is that we cannot compare Him with anything or anyone. He is incomparable.

One of our difficulties is in trying to define God. I believe that in the Scriptures God gives us leeway in this area because there are no words to exactly describe and define God. He is beyond definition and description. Yet there is a desire on our part to know God and to follow after Him. What we know about God is really just a sliver of who God really is.

We have to try to organize what we know into little pigeonholes. That is for our benefit, not God's. You cannot put God in a pigeonhole. Whatever God is, He is all the time. When we think of the attributes of God, we study them individually, but with God there is no dividing of one attribute from another.

Whatever God is, He is. When we talk about the unity of God and His attributes, we sometimes think of all of the parts of God working together harmoniously. That is an inadequate picture of God. God is not made up of parts. God is God. A man of God wisely once said that God's attributes are numberless. We can know a few of God's attributes; and an attribute, as I have explained many times, is what God has revealed about himself to be true.

Our problem comes when we try to understand God. We work piece by piece, and then we try to put all the pieces together. Again, God gives us leeway in this area. He knows how limited we are. But as limited as we are, God is unlimited.

Take the human body, for example. Health for us is when all our parts are working together harmoniously. When one of our organs is out of alignment with our other organs, we have some physical issues. Everything must work together. Yet some people are missing some internal organs and still live. There are some who have had heart transplants and are living because of that. Because we are made up of parts, we have health issues.

Our problem is when we take this human experience and place it on our understanding of God.

When we say that God is a God of love, what we mean many times is that God does not hate. Yet there are many Scriptures that tell us about the anger and hate of God toward sin and the sinner. This does not mean that God's love works at one time and then, changing gears, His hate works at another time. Changing gears may work in an automobile, but it does not work with God. God has no gears to change.

God is what He is in one harmonious unity of uncreation.

Now, because of the unity of God, there is no limit to whatever God is. For example, there is no limit to His mercy. God is as merciful to one person as He is to another. On the other hand, what about God's grace? God's grace is just as available to one person as it is to another person. The fact that some people are not experiencing the mercy and grace of God in their personal experience is not God's fault. God made a way for us to experience Him in all His fullness, and that way is none other than the Lord Jesus Christ, who said, "I am the way" (John 14:6).

There is no limit to the goodness of God. God is as good to one person as He is to another. Experiencing that goodness on a human level is our challenge. We can experience as much of God's goodness as we are willing to experience. God does not set a limit on how much of His goodness or His grace or His mercy or His love we can experience.

The more we delve into the beauty of God, the more we are surrounded by an unlimited sense of His beauty. God wants to declare this beauty upon our lives. God wants to pour into us the unlimitedness of all of His attributes and nature and character. Our problem is our limitation determines how much of God we can experience.

The thing that I have discovered is simply this: The more I experience God, the more my capacity to experience God grows. Each day as I walk with God and allow the Holy Spirit to reveal to me who God really is, the more my capacity grows in worshiping and adoring this God.

What this means is that my worship grows and grows as my perception of God grows. God cannot grow. My perception of God grows as I experience Him day after day. I should be more capable of worshiping God today than I was ten or twenty years ago. As I move toward God, my capacity to understand God grows deeper and deeper.

Of course, the opposite is also true. As I move away from God, my capacity begins to shrink. How many Christians are experiencing a shrinking capacity to worship God? Perhaps that is the reason why our music today is so superficial.

Zion, On the Holy Hills

Zion, on the holy hills,

God, thy Maker, loves thee well;

All thy courts His presence fills,

He delights in thee to dwell.

Wondrous shall thy glory be,

City blest of God, the Lord;

Nations shall be born in thee,

Unto life from death restored.

When the Lord the names shall write

Of thy sons, a countless throng,

God Most High will thee requite,

He himself will make thee strong.

Then in song and joyful mirth

Shall thy ransomed sons agree,

Singing forth throughout the earth,

"All my fountains are in thee."

The Psalter

Chapter 6
Reasons for a Faulty Perception of God

O God, we often fall into the trap of assuming we are right with Thee when the reality is, we are far from Thee. Stir up our hearts that we will not be content with where we are or what we have, but that our contentment will be focused only in Thee. Amen.

Our perception of God is so crucial that great pains must be taken to make sure it is deeply rooted in the foundation of God's Word. It is quite easy to get sidetracked and try to update God's Word. God's Word to Moses is our word today: Do not change the plan I gave you on the mountain. We are guilty sometimes of changing God's plan because, for some reason, we think we know better than God.

Several things need to be dealt with if we are going to keep our perception of God where it needs to be. There are certain things that we do that are detrimental to our spiritual progress. Let me outline a few of the mistakes we make that hinder our progress.

I think the first mistake is assuming that because it is in the Bible, it is in us.

Someone in a prayer meeting gets up and gives a testimony: "I am crucified with Christ: nevertheless I live; yet not I, but Christ liveth in me; and the life which I now live in the flesh I live by the faith of the Son of God, who loved me, and gave himself for me" (Galatians 2:20).

Because he quoted Scripture and believes in the Scriptures, he assumes that what the Scripture says is a reality in his own life. But the man who gives this kind of testimony may not have much in his life that really supports and substantiates this testimony. Because you believe it does not mean it is a reality in your life. We assume that if it is in the Bible, it is in us.

For myself, if it is not in the Bible, I do not want it in me. It can, however, be in the Bible and never get in me at all. Because our Bible teachers often lead us down this road, we assume that if we read it in the Bible, it is in us, whether or not we have appropriated it.

It will not take five minutes in the actual presence of the Lord Jesus Christ to bring tears to our eyes when we realize what we missed while here on earth. We will see how we were betrayed by those who pretended to be teaching us but left us hanging high and dry. The Lord meant that we should be the happiest, fullest, most overflowing people in the world.

We can have everything the Bible tells us we can have, but we cannot assume that we have it because the Bible says it. We must come to the point of personally experiencing everything that the Bible is teaching us. To know the first step is important, but it is only the first step, and we must persevere unto perfection; that is, experiencing what God wants us to experience in the Lord Jesus Christ by the power of the Holy Spirit.

Another mistake that hinders our perception of God is just plain spiritual laziness. That sounds harsh, but I have seen it all around, even in my own life. Physical laziness is one thing, but spiritual laziness is something we never really deal with in our lives.

We can make ourselves do physical exercise to compensate for physical laziness, but it is almost impossible to make ourselves do some intellectual exercise. The average church today is geared to the level of a home for backward children. The pastor does not dare rise into high theology, because his poor backward sheep cannot follow him. It is hard to get people to think, but it is harder still to get them to thirst.

We can encourage people to exercise physically, and they will see immediate results if they work at it hard enough. And we can get a few to exercise intellectually. But when it comes to making people spiritually thirsty, it takes the Holy Spirit to do that. I have discovered that the frustrating aspect of preaching and teaching is that the preacher and teacher cannot do the work of change for people. It must be a work of the Holy Spirit within the heart of the believer. I can encourage people to read books, but I cannot talk people into a hunger and thirst for the things of God. It takes the Holy Spirit to do that.

Another mistake that hinders and compromises our perception of God is our love of the world. By this, I mean that we accept the prevailing standard in the world to be "normal."

Say a child is born in a sanitarium for tuberculosis patients. It sounds ridiculous, but bear with me. That child is born there, lives there, grows up there, and accepts the situation he is in as normal—he does not know any better. Everyone has a cough, everyone holds his chest, everyone carries a little bag to spit in, everyone has to take five naps a day and live on a special diet. If you are brought up in that environment, you think it is normal and you adjust your whole life to that normality.

So it is possible to be brought up in a church today, accept the low, weak, anemic, worn-out type of Christianity there, believe it is New Testament Christianity, and expect nothing better—that there's nothing more to look for.

When the world is our model for normality, we become adjusted to the world's standards. When we become adjusted to the world's standards, we are at odds with the Word's standards. Everything seems normal, and nobody suspects that there is something more to be grasped as far as the Christian life is concerned.

Remember, it is the Holy Spirit who commands us to press on to perfection. This is a matter of daily spiritual discipline.

I think another mistake we make that really affects our perception of God is our overall eagerness to be consoled, no matter what. Do we come to a point in the church where consolation is our God?

Some go to church looking for consolation. We are encouraged to go to church to find peace and consolation. But the church is not a place to find consolation; it is a place to hear the gospel preached so you can find salvation. A big difference exists between being consoled and being saved. A man can find consolation and end up finally in hell. A man can be under blistering, terrifying conviction, get converted, and go finally to heaven.

We demand that our preachers console us all the time. We want to be consoled and comforted as though we were little boys and girls. Personally, I want to know the worst about myself now so I can do something about it while there is still time. If I do not know what is wrong, I will never be able to correct it, which will have an adverse effect on my life.

Another drastic mistake, which I will touch on later in this book, is an unwillingness to die to the flesh.

I wrote some articles for a Christian magazine on the subject of the Holy Spirit. The theme of those articles had to do with our deeper life and our relationship with the Holy Spirit. This series of articles created two reactions, different as night from day.

The series consisted of four articles, and when the last of the articles was published, I received a very long letter from a well-known Bible expositor. In that letter he said that after he read my article, he was distressed because he felt I was leading people astray. Did I not know, he said, that everyone who was a believer had the Holy Spirit, and did I not know that the command to be filled with the Spirit was not something ever intended for us to obey, but rather an ideal set before us? It was only something to keep us moving, but the idea that God should ever fill anybody with the Holy Spirit just could not be. He included some other items in that letter.

I laid the letter aside and never replied to it. You cannot change the thinking of some people. Then I received another letter from the same person informing me that he had been disappointed in not getting a reply. "I want a reply," he demanded.

So I replied:

Dear brother, I had not meant to be discourteous in not replying to your letter, but there are some things too scared to expose to the unsympathetic gaze of a man who believes as you do. Second, I hope you will not think me uncharitable if I say that if God's people were as eager to be filled with the Holy Spirit as they are to prove that you cannot be, the church might come out of her doldrums.

He wrote again with a copy of my letter enclosed and said he was sending this letter and one of his own to the editor of the magazine, demanding equal space to answer me. He just was not going to let it alone, that anybody could be filled with the Holy Spirit.

Letters like that can be depressing, but then I got another letter from the editor of that magazine.

He was riding the train out of Chicago and happened to sit beside a fine-looking young fellow, perhaps in his late twenties, and he got into a conversation. After introductions, the young man said, "I have heard about that magazine." And they discussed many things and finally got around to discussing the articles I had written on the Holy Spirit.

"I have been reading those articles on the deeper life," he said, "and I do not know, but I am just sick. I do not think I am even converted. It is awful. I have suffered, and I have gone through so much, and I just do not know. I want to be filled with the Holy Spirit. This is an awful state that I am in."

My friend arrived at his station and got off, so they parted ways. Some months went by and they met again on the train, and the young man remembered my friend. This time my friend noticed that the gloom was all gone. The young man's face was shining like the morning sun after the rain.

After their introductory greeting, my friend said, "The last time I saw you, you had a long face. You were in misery."

"Yes," he said, "but do you know what? God met me. God met me! Now I want to tell you about something. I want you to pray for me; I have a decision to make. I was just in Europe under the auspices of the World Council of Churches, and I saw the poor sheep looking so poorly. I gave a speech at this great convention, and I was bubbling over with God. I do not know why I said it, but I closed my speech by saying, 'Have you received the Holy Spirit since you believed?' I sat down and some old preachers came around and said, 'Young fellow, thank God you dared to say that. We believe it but are afraid to say it.'"

Then he said to my friend, "I want you to pray for me. I have to make up my mind whether I can stay in that denomination any longer or not."

Two people, the same series of articles on the Holy Spirit, and two completely difference responses. One man was red hot and determined to prove that you cannot be filled with the Holy Spirit. Another man, out of a dead denomination, got so blistering hot under conviction that he found God without anyone to help him and dared to shock the gathering of the World Council of Churches.

This is the difference between a hungry man and one who is satisfied. Now, the question that I must ask, not only of myself, but of you as a reader is this: Are you satisfied, or are you hungry?

The answer to that one question will point you in one direction or another. And the answer to that question and the follow-through of that question will greatly determine your perception of God.

If you are hungry enough to do something about it, you will have climbed high on the mountain of God. If you are satisfied, you will be the same mediocre weakling that you are right now. It is just a question of how bad you want to know God.

Thy Way, Not Mine, O Lord

Thy way, not mine, O Lord,

However dark it be!

Lead me by Thine own hand,

Choose out the path for me.

Smooth let it be or rough,

It will be still the best;

Winding or straight, it matters not,

Right onward to Thy rest.

I dare not choose my lot;

I would not, if I might;

Choose Thou for me, my God;

So I shall walk aright.

The kingdom that I seek
Is Thine: so let the way
That leads to it be Thine,
Else I must surely stray.

Take Thou my cup, and it
With joy or sorrow fill,
As best to Thee may seem;
Choose Thou my good and ill.

Choose Thou for me my friends,
My sickness or my health;
Choose Thou my cares for me,
My poverty or wealth.

Not mine, not mine the choice
In things both great or small;
Be Thou my guide, my strength,
My wisdom, and my all.
Horatius Bonar
(1808–1889)

Chapter 7

The Perception of Our Relationship with God

Dear Lord Jesus, I long to know Thee, and fellowship with Thee, and draw near unto the mystery of Thy Majesty. Open up my heart to see what Thou wouldst want me to see as far as my relationship with Thee goes. Fill my heart with wondrous expectation rooted in the heart of the Lord Jesus Christ. Amen.

Before we go any further, we need to look at who Christ is and what His relationship is to the redeemed company, which we call the church. Who is this Christ? How do I relate to this Christ? All of this needs to be answered in a way that will draw me into the heart of God. It is one thing to have a lot of information about God, but it is another thing to bask in the warmth and reality of His presence.

Our relationship to God can be condensed, rather imperfectly, into three words: centrality, "basicality," and preeminence. These three words, if understood in the context of Scripture, will bring great enlightenment into the heart of the believer. We are part of Christ, but I believe it goes much deeper than that.

Jesus Christ is Central

The old devotional writers used to emphasize that Christ is to the church what the soul is to the body. You know what the soul is to the body; it is that which gives it life, and when the soul flees the body, it cannot keep the body alive. When the soul is gone, then the embalmer takes over, and in the church of Christ—any church, anywhere, of any denomination, whatever it may call itself—as long as Christ is there, imparting life to that redeemed company, you have the church. Christ is central in His church. He holds it together, and in Him it appears.

Jesus Christ is Basic

The next word is basicality. I do not think there is such a word; I made it up. But if there is not such a word, there ought to be. What I mean is that Jesus Christ is basic to the church. He is underneath it, and the whole redeemed company rests on the Lord Jesus Christ. I think I might be able to go around the world and simply cry, "Christ is enough."

What weakens us in evangelical circles is that we put a plus sign after Christ. Christ plus something else. It is always the pluses that ruin our spiritual lives. It is always the additions, or the additives, as we say now, that weaken the church. Remember that God has declared that His Son, Christ, is sufficient. He is the way, the truth, and the life; He is wisdom, righteousness, sanctification, and redemption. He is the wisdom of God and the power of God that gathers onto himself all things, and in Him all things consist so that we do not want Jesus Christ plus something else, or Jesus Christ and something else. We must never put an end after Christ, waiting for something else, or Christ with a dash, leading to something else. We must preach Christ, for Christ is enough.

We of the evangelical faith—which is, I believe and have always believed, to be the faith of our fathers and the biblical faith—should not put Christ plus science or Christ plus philosophy or Christ plus psychology or Christ plus education or Christ plus anything else, but Christ alone. These other things may have their place and be used, just as you can throw sand into vats where they are making glass and it will all melt. We can use all these things, but we are not leaning on any of them. We are resting on Him who is basic to the faith of our fathers.

Christ is Preeminent

Then we have the word preeminent—that Christ might be preeminent and placed above all things. Let us think of Jesus Christ above all things, underneath all things, outside of all things, and inside of all things. He is above all things but not pushed up. He is beneath all things but not pressed down. He is outside of all things but not excluded, and inside but not confined. He is above all presiding, beneath all upholding, outside of all embracing, and inside of all building.

We are committed to Jesus Christ, our Lord, alone. Our relationship to Christ is all that matters, really. I believe that a true Christian's faith is an attachment to the person of Christ in total commitment to Him.

Several things are involved in this attachment to the person of Jesus Christ.

There is an intellectual attachment. To follow Jesus Christ forward in complete commitment, total commitment, means there has to be an intellectual attachment to Christ; that is, we cannot run on our feelings or wisps of poetic notions about Christ. We have a good many bogus Christ's among us these days, and I believe that as followers of the Lamb, we are obligated to point out these bogus Christ's, show them up for what they are, and then point to the Lamb of God that takes away the sin of the world.

We must warn people today that if they have an imaginary Christ and are satisfied with an imaginary Christ, then they must be satisfied with an imaginary salvation. That seems to be the bottom line with us. Our salvation is no better than our perception of Christ. If that perception is flawed, our salvation is also flawed.

In our world today, there are many Christ's, many Lords, and many Gods. We have a knack for dreaming up a God of our imagination that satisfies us at the time. However, our message is that there is only one Christ, and those who follow Christ have an attachment to Him that is an intellectual attachment, that is, they know Christ theologically.

There is the romantic Christ of the female novelist, the sentimental Christ of the half-converted cowboy, the philosophical Christ of the academic egghead, the cozy Christ of the effeminate poet, and the muscular Christ of the all-American athlete. We have these kinds of Christ's, but there is only one Christ, and God has said about Him that He is His Son.

The Athanasian Creed says that "Lord Jesus Christ, the Son of God, is God and man: God of the substance of the Father, begotten before the worlds; a man of substance of His mother, born in the world; perfect God and perfect man, subsisting of a reasonable soul and human flesh; equal to the Father as touching His divinity, and inferior to the Father as touching His manhood, who, although He is God and man, yet He is not two, but one Christ." This is the Christ we adore, and we must have knowledge of this; that is, we must have the Christ of Christian theology.

I would never have anything to do with any book or any movement or any religion or any emphasis that does not begin with Christ, go out from Christ, and return to Christ again—the Christ of God, the Christ of the Bible, the Christ of Christian theology, the historic Christ of the Scriptures. He is the One, so we must have an intellectual attachment to Christ. You cannot simply let your heart run out to Christ with some kind of warm feelings about Him and not be sure of who He is. This is the essence of heresy.

We must believe in the Christ of God; we must believe in who God said He is.

Volitional Attachment to Christ

Then there is the volitional attachment to Christ. If I am going to follow Christ forward in complete and total commitment, I must do it by my will. A person is in bad shape and is making a grave mistake when he tries to live on impulse, inspiration, and feelings. The man who lives on his feelings is not doing very well and is not going to be able to last very long. The old devotional writers used to tell of "the dark night of the soul." There is a place where the Christian goes through darkness, where there is heaviness.

Some believe that God is going to take us off to heaven all wrapped up in cellophane, looking like we ought to be hanging on the Christmas tree. God is going to take us to heaven after He has purged us and disciplined us and taken us through the fire and has made us strong. Thank God that faith brings feeling, as they used to sing:

O Happy Day, that Fixed My Choice

O happy day, that fixed my choice

On Thee, my Savior and my God!

Well may this glowing heart rejoice,

And tell its raptures all abroad.

O happy bond, that seals my vows

To Him who merits all my love!

Let cheerful anthems fill His house,

While to that sacred shrine I move.

Now rest, my long divided heart,

Fixed on this blissful center, rest.

Here have I found a nobler part;

Here heavenly pleasures fill my breast.

High heaven, that heard the solemn vow,

That vow renewed shall daily hear,

Till in life's latest hour I bow

And bless in death a bond so dear.

Philip Doddridge

(1702–1751)

People are afraid to pray those words now. I believe that just as Daniel determined that he would not eat of the king's meat, and just as Jesus set His face like a flint, and just as Paul said, "This one thing I do," I believe true followers of Christ must be people whose wills have been sanctified, not men and women without wills. I never believed that when we teach the deeper life, we are to say that God destroys our will. A man would be of no good in the world, and you would have to put him in traction to hold him up. If you have no will, you have no purpose. The beautiful thing is that God unites our will with His will, and our will becomes strong; and His will merges us with God so that we hardly know if it is our will or God's will that is working at any given moment.

Our Exclusive Attachment to Christ

Our attachment to the person of Christ must exclude everything that is contrary to Christ. There is a polarity in the Christian life, and this polarization begins at the very threshold of that life.

We live in a time when we are trying to be 100 percent positive. But the Scriptures say that God loves righteousness and hates iniquity. It also says that Christ himself is higher than the highest heavens, separate from sinners. If He had to hate in order to love, so do you and I.

We are told today to be positive. People often write to tell me that I am negative and encourage me to go positive. To be positive 100 percent of the time would be as futile and as useless and, thank God, as fatal as to inhale steadily all your life without exhaling. The human body requires that you inhale to get oxygen and exhale to get rid of the poisons. So the church of Christ must inhale and exhale. When she inhales, she must exhale, and when the church of Christ inhales the Holy Spirit, she must exhale everything contrary to Him.

Some churches wonder why the Holy Spirit has not been around since last Christmas. The reason is they have not exhaled. They have not gotten rid of the old businesses in there. I do not believe that any man is able to love until he is able to hate. I do not think any man can love God unless he hates the devil. I do not think he can love righteousness unless he hates sin. The Scriptures leave us with the opinion, with the belief, that in order to accept, there are some things we need to reject. In order to own, you must repudiate some things. In order to affirm, there are some things you must deny. In order to say yes, you have to be able to say no. The man who does not have the courage or the intestinal fortitude to roar a thundering no to some things can never say yes and make it mean anything.

I, for my part, have come to the conclusion that I cannot get along with everybody. The idea of soft-handed pastors with a saintly flush on their faces, trying to get along with everybody, will not do. In an effort to please everybody, we succeed in pleasing nobody. We are tempted to try to keep from offending anybody. I do not want to water down Christianity. I want to be able to say no and mean it. I want to be able to say no to the wrong things and yes to the right things.

An Inclusive Attachment to Christ

This is the inhaling, you see. All that Christ is and does and says and promises and commands, and all the glories that circle around His head, and all the offices He holds, and all the shining beauty of the various facets of His infinite nature, all that He is, all that He has said, all that He has promised, I take that all. I include it all.

I am joining Christ and identifying with Him. So I accept His friends as my friends. I love all the people of God. I believe God has His children everywhere, and all God's children have wings, and so I love them all.

I accept God's friends as my friends. And in turn, I accept His enemies as my enemies. An old bishop once said that the Lord has His treasures in earthen vessels, and some of those vessels are a bit cracked. I need to be willing to own the friends of the Lord, wherever they are and whoever they are. His friends are my friends, and His enemies are my enemies.

What would be a good definition of a Christian? A good definition of a Christian is someone who is back from the dead. I think Paul was one of the oddest and strangest, and one of the most glorious, of anyone who ever lived. Paul gave us a text that seems to be a little odd: "I am crucified with Christ: nevertheless I live" (Galatians 2:20). How did Paul get that way? He is dead and then he is alive. Is he dead or is he alive? He goes on to say, "And the life which I now live in the flesh I live by the faith of the Son of God, who loved me, and gave himself for me." Paul is contradicting himself, and yet with all the contradiction, there is a marvelous and glorious truth.

A Christian is one who was crucified and yet is alive, being joined to Jesus Christ. All members of the body of Christ are joined to His body and share in some measure in that hypostatic union of God and man. We are united with Him, so when He died on the cross and rose from the dead, we also rose from the dead. When He went to the right hand of God the Father, we went to the right hand of God the Father. If any man be in Christ, he seeks those things that are above. And as it is written, we sit in the heavenly places, which means that we are really where He is, and we are members of His great mystical body.

Our Irrevocable Attachment to Christ

By this I mean that the Lord does not want any experimenters. Someone wrote a book once called Try Jesus. All this experimentation—I do not believe in it.

A young man came to an old saint and asked him, "What does it mean to be crucified with Christ?"

After thinking for a moment, the old saint said, "To be crucified means three things. First, the man who is crucified is facing in only one direction. You cannot turn around to see what is going on behind you. You stopped looking back and look straight ahead. The man on the cross is looking in only one direction, and that is the direction of God, Christ, and the Holy Spirit, in the direction of biblical revelation, of angels, and edifying of the church, the direction of sanctification and the Spirit-filled life. He is looking only in one direction."

Then the old man thought for a moment and said, "One thing more about a man on a cross; he is not going back. The man going out to die on a cross does not say to his wife, 'Good-bye, honey. I will be in shortly after five.' He is not coming back.

When you go out to die on a cross, you say good-bye to your friends, you kiss your friends good-bye, and you are not coming back." I think if we would teach more of this and stop trying to make the Christian life so easy that it is contemptible, we would have more converts that would last. Get a man to know he is joining Christ and is finished as far as this world is concerned, and he is not going back, and he has to take a cross on the shoulder.

"Another thing about the man on a cross," said the man, "he has no further plans of his own. Someone else has made his plans for him. On the way up the hill, he does not see a friend and say to him, 'Well, Henry, next Saturday afternoon about three we'll go fishing up by the lake.' He is not going fishing. He is finished. He is going out to die; he has no plans at all."

We are busy-beaver Christians with all our plans. Even though some plans are done in the name of the Lord and evangelical Christianity, they are as carnal as goats. It depends on who is making your plans for you.

It is beautiful to say, "I am crucified with Christ" and know that Christ is making your plans. Twenty minutes on your knees in silence before God will sometimes teach you more than you can learn out of books and teach you more than you can learn even in the church. God will give you your plans and lay them before you. We could cut down our time of debating and discussing if we would spend more time waiting on God. We are to be joined to Christ intellectually, volitionally, and exclusively so that we become expendable and do not go back.

Forward!

Christ, our mighty captain, leads against the foe,

We will never falter when He bids us go;

Tho' His righteous purpose we may never know,

Yet we'll follow all the way.

Refrain:

Forward! forward! 'tis the Lord's command;

Forward! forward! to the promised land;

Forward! forward! let the chorus ring:

We are sure to win with Christ, our King!

Satan's fearful onslaughts cannot make us yield;

While we trust in Christ, our buckler and our shield;

Pressing ever on—the Spirit's sword we wield,

And we follow all the way.

Let our glorious banner ever be unfurled;
From its mighty stronghold evil shall be hurled;
Christ, our mighty Captain, overcomes the world,
And we follow all the way.

Fierce the battle rages—but 'twill not be long,
Then triumphant, shall we join the bless'ed throng,
Joyfully uniting in the victor's song—
If we follow all the way.
Carrie E. Breck
(1855–1934)

Chapter 8
Our Perception of God Determines Everything

Our Father, which art in heaven, how wondrous the world as seen through Thine eyes. The more we come to know Thee, the more we begin to understand the creative world around us and above us. Thou hast built the world to honor Thee in every possible way. Every aspect of the world reveals something of Thy character and nature. May I discover more of that perception today through Jesus Christ. Amen.

When our perception of God has been damaged or compromised, everything around us falls into confusion and turmoil. Nothing seems to make sense, and everything seems to be at odds with one another. This, as I have pointed out, is a result of man's downfall in the garden of Eden. The whole created world was affected by this.

"For we know," Paul writes, "that the whole creation groaneth and travaileth in pain together until now" (Romans 8:22). It is not possible for us to know what this world was like prior to the curse of sin. One day we shall experience that, but until then, we are laboring under this terrible curse affecting all humanity and all creation. By getting to know God, I begin to understand how things are supposed to be. My perception of God is the foundation of my understanding of everything else. Once I know who God is and that He is the Creator and Redeemer, I begin to look at things quite differently.

By nature, I would be considered by many a pessimist. I can look around and see everything that is wrong. When I begin to understand God, my pessimism begins to change to optimism. My nature has been corrupted by depravity, but my new nature in Christ elevates me above the depravity level and introduces me into the glory level. I begin to see the world through divine eyes. The divine perspective, if you please, has affected everything in my life.

In my younger days, I had a deep appreciation for classical music. I enjoyed listening to it and could identify all the major classical musicians. I had great times debating who was the best classical musician and composer. Those days are behind me now. It is not because I have grown older; it is because I have grown nearer to God. All of the beauty of that secular music and the brilliance of the composers began to fade in comparison to a simple hymn.

I readily admit most hymns cannot compare in brilliance to the great classical composers. Most hymns have flaws in the areas of composition and music. The hymn writers are not in the same class as the great composers of classical music. I get that.

However, as my relationship with God has deepened and I have gotten closer to God, something has changed within me. I no longer look at music in the same way. I am not looking for brilliance in music or composition anymore. My appreciation of hymnody has grown.

I think my attraction to hymns has to do with why and how that hymn came about. I know that the great hymn writers did not write to impress the listening audience, but out of a heart deeply worshiping God. The worship aspect has attracted me. In the classical compositions, I was worshiping the composition. Now the great hymns of the church have brought me to the place of lifting myself into the presence of God. A hymn is not a hymn unless it lifts me into that rarefied atmosphere of adoring wonder and worship of God.

I may be able to appreciate secular music, but as I have grown in Christ, it does not have the same effect on me as it once did. My heart is stirred to levels of adoration that no secular piece of music can give me when I am reflecting upon one of the grand hymns of the church.

I believe that is why the Twenty-third Psalm is so beautiful—because it honors God. And I think that goes with the whole Bible itself. This book I hold in my hand is a shining, beautiful book. It is lovely no matter whether it is bound in the cheapest of paper or in the most expensive leather, whether it is printed on plain paper or the finest India paper available; nevertheless, it is a beautiful book.

When it comes to the Bible, I have grown a little weary of the battle about translations: which translation is better, which is more accurate, which is more scholarly. I have in my library every translation of the Bible available today. I love the Bible, and in spite of all of these translations—and many are wonderful—I find myself gravitating back to the good old King James Version. This is not because it is any better as far as a translation is concerned, but there is something in this Bible that stirs my heart and lifts me above the intellectual realm into the realm of adoration. If after reading and meditating on the Bible, I have not encountered the Living Word, I have truly read in vain. In my reading of God's Word, I need to persist until I pierce the darkness and come into the light of His presence.

As I meditate on the Word of God, my heart is stirred, and my concept of the Bible is a direct result of my growing appreciation of God. The more I know God, the more I understand His character and nature. The more I delve into the attributes of God and the more I meditate upon His Word, the more I begin to appreciate everything around me. My relationship with God through Jesus Christ has given me new glasses from which I can look upon the world in deep appreciation and see what God intends for me to see.

I think Christianity is the most beautiful thing in the world. I think the Bible is the most beautiful book in the world. I think a good hymnbook is the most awesome, wonderful, beautiful thing in the world. And I think the face of an old saint is more beautiful than all the composite beauty of all the bathing beauties.

As we move toward God, all things become more beautiful, and as we move away from God, they become uglier. This is why theology is a beautiful thing. Theology is simply the study of God. It is the mind reasoning about God. It is the mind kneeling before God in meditative worship of God.

This kind of theology can be beautiful if it begins in God and ends in God. That is the secret. I know there are those so-called theologians who have spun theology into some technical composite of religious matters. Let them be as they are. My concept of theology is God. I want to know God. The more I know God, the more my heart is filled with worship and adoration. As I grow nearer to God, I discover the beauty of all things pertaining to God. I believe worship is admiring the beauty associated with God. If our theology is not full of beauty, it is simply because it is not full of God. Nothing about God is ugly. The closer we get to God, the more we appreciate what beauty is all about. When we begin moving away from God, we begin to experience the ugliness that is in the world.

This affects our concept of heaven and hell and even the earth. Some of the things being published today about heaven are so off-center with the Word of God, I wonder where they come up with those ideas. Heaven is not a fictional place of fantasy and folklore; neither is hell.

Our Concept of Heaven

Heaven is the place of supreme beauty because perfection is there. The perfect God, the God of unqualified beauty—He is there, and heaven is going to be beautiful. Our problem today is we are too satisfied with earth. After all, with a split-level house, a TV, and two cars, why would you want to go to heaven? There is no good reason for going to heaven if everything is so nice down here. Nobody chases you and comes at midnight and puts you in jail. Nobody comes and locks up your church and persecutes you. We have it too nice down here. We have it all fixed up. Henry Ford and Thomas Edison and others fixed it all up for us so we can be born in a hospital and go home, and never get off the sidewalk and live our lifetime on concrete, and die in the hospital and be taken to Memorial Park, and packed away among the artificial green grass. It is a beautiful place we live in, you know, if you see it from above eye view. It is quite a beautiful place, this world; why should you want to go to heaven?

We sing about heaven an awful lot, not because we expect to get there ahead of the rest, but just because we think heaven must be a wonderful place if Jesus Christ is there. The beautiful One, the Lord of glory, the One altogether lovely—if He is there, it must be a wonderful place.

I am convinced that the average Christian needs to rethink their concept of heaven. Much of their idea of heaven has come from the world, the best things of the world projected upward into a place called heaven. Nothing could be more discouraging, if you think it through carefully. Heaven is not the best the world has to offer. Heaven is the best God has to offer. The more we begin to know God and understand His character and nature, the more we will begin to understand what heaven is all about.

A lot of literature has been published concerning heaven and what people think it will be like. It is amazing that someone who will live a life of depravity here on earth expects to go to heaven when they die. Their life is filled with the ugliness of the world, but somehow they believe they will go zooming off to heaven when they die. After all, everybody goes to heaven. At least that is what they are told.

I think we need to see what the Bible has to say about heaven and not what somebody out in the world has to say about it.

If a person, for example, was going on a vacation, they would get as much information about their vacation destination as possible. They would want to see brochures and maps and literature to understand a little bit about what to expect when they get there. I think the same needs to be true concerning heaven.

What is Heaven All About?

If you could imagine the most beautiful thing here on earth, it has no comparison to the beauty of heaven. We need to understand that earth, this world about us, is under the curse of sin. Heaven will be absolutely free from all aspects of sin. That is difficult for us who have groaned under the weight of depravity to appreciate.

As Christians, we need to cultivate a more heavenly mind. It is easy to get so caught up with the world around us that we fail to look and see the beauty of our Lord.

The hymn writer Samuel Stennett wrote of the essence of this in his hymn:

On Jordan's stormy banks I stand,

And cast a wistful eye

To Canaan's fair and happy land,

Where my possessions lie.

Stennett understood how stormy this world really was and that there was nothing here for him. Can we appreciate the beauty of heaven? In the midst of all the "stormy banks" do we take the time to "cast a wistful eye" to that "fair and happy land"? Ah, the beauty of heaven is beyond our ability to describe or even appreciate now.

I refuse to read a book written by someone who knows more about heaven than the Bible tells us. If we get our information about heaven from sources other than the Bible, we are not going to get a view of heaven as God has it. There is so much about heaven that we do not know.

For example, I do not know where heaven is. Sometimes people look up into the air as though heaven were above them. Perhaps it is—I do not know. Not knowing where heaven is not as important as knowing that heaven is my destination.

The technology of our generation has advanced to such a point that we can send rockets up into the air for thousands of miles. Some wonder if maybe we are now getting closer to heaven. I do not know where heaven is, but I do know that you cannot get there on the most sophisticated technological rocket man could ever create. Man does not have the capacity to build his own pathway into heaven. Remember the Tower of Babel? For one thing, he does not know where heaven is. For another thing, what would it take to get to heaven?

With all of man's ingenuity, he has yet to build the doorway into heaven. "I am the way," Jesus said to His disciples, "the truth, and the life: no man cometh unto the Father, but by me" (John 14:6). If we are going to get into God's heaven, it is going to be by God's way. For me, I want nothing at all to do with man's heaven or man's idea of heaven or man's perception of heaven. I have seen what man has done here on earth, and I do not want any of it to get into heaven.

Heaven is God's domain, and it has all about it the beauty of God's nature. Heaven is a reflection of all the attributes of God and His nature and character. It is a place where God is most comfortable and a place where God's people will find peace and tranquility.

What we see here on earth is nothing compared to what we will see in heaven. After all, what does the world really have to offer us? We are here for only a short time anyway. The best the world has to offer is temporary. The world tries to tempt us with gadgets and products that will bring us satisfaction, but it does so only temporarily. What God has for us is something that will last for all eternity.

Our Concept of Hell

Once we get a slight understanding—which is as much as we can do—of heaven, we need to turn our attention to hell. We do not like to talk about hell anymore. We would much rather talk about heaven. I know I would, but the truth of the matter is, there is indeed a hell to avoid. Our problem today is we do not have a realistic view of hell.

There is nothing beautiful about hell as there is about heaven. In hell, we find only monstrous moral deformity and depravity and monstrous ugliness. Some wonder about the fire of hell. The Bible is clear concerning the fire in hell and the lake of fire. But just for a moment, forget about the fire. Hell has such an ugliness about it that it is reported by anyone who looks into it.

The Bible clearly declares hell was made for the devil and his demons. Hell is not a place for man. Man was created for heaven. But when sin came into the world and tarnished the image of God within man, he became disqualified for heaven. The only place that could receive him following his death was hell.

When people say a man is lost, that lostness will never be more in view than when that person actually goes to hell. He will be in a place in which he is out of place. Nothing in hell will do anything for the person in hell.

Think for a moment of a place where there is no beauty, no perfection of wisdom, no understanding of God's nature—a place of ugliness beyond anything we know here on earth. Think of the ugliest place on earth, the most morally depraved place on earth, and it is nothing compared to the ugliness of hell.

William Booth, founder of the Salvation Army, was a very passive Christian until he had a vision of hell. That vision so stirred him that he spent the rest of his life rescuing as many people as possible from that awful and terrible destination.

If we only understood what hell was all about, we would become the fieriest evangelists of our generation.

Our Concept of the Earth

After we have seen the contrast between heaven and hell, we need to correct our perception of earth.

Heaven is a place of utter beauty, whereas hell is a place of utter depravity. Earth now falls halfway between heaven and hell. There are aspects of earth that are simply beautiful. There are also aspects of earth that are absolutely ugly.

To understand the contradiction here on earth, we need to get a good view of heaven and hell. We need to see that here on earth is the great battleground between heaven and hell. If I am not careful, I am tempted to believe that hell is winning.

It is easy to see the ugliness permeating through our world today. The depravity of man is raging in our generation like never before. The ability of man to be wicked, hateful, and murderous is a picture of earth's ugliness. We see what man is capable of and how sin rules the day, making this world a dreadful place to live. Regardless of what governments try to do, the sin nature is on a rampage and will not cease until the end of time.

In contrast to this is the beauty of the earth. There are some things that are reflecting the beauty of our Creator. Redeemed men and women are reflecting into their communities the beauty of our Lord in a way that gives testimony to God's grace. The beauty of godly living can be seen as a contrast to the depravity in our world today.

What is the responsibility of the church today? The first obligation that lies on current Christianity is to go back to God and get to know God as He is revealed in the Scriptures: Father, Son, and Holy Spirit. He is terrible and wonderful and beautiful and lovely and just and severe and kind and holy and pure. You cannot joke with or fool with or pal around with God. He is the awesome God of our fathers whose almighty hand leads forth in beauty all the starry band. The first duty of every minister of the gospel is to bring God back to the church—not the intellectual God of the academics, not the palsy God of the gospelers, not the chairman of the board, but the God who reveals himself in the Scriptures and who revealed himself supremely in the person of the Lord Jesus Christ.

That God must be recaptured—that perception of God must be recaptured. We must bring God back again into our fellowship, the triune God. We must cease to fool with little things, all the little things that we are doing, forgetting that we have one awful loss: the loss of our perception of a majestic God who is worthy to be worshiped.

God made us in His image and never meant for us to mirror anything less than himself. He never meant for us to have a homemade perception of God. There are two kinds of idolatry. It may be overt idolatry, where men make an idol and kneel before it. That is at least honest. But there is another kind of idolatry, and it is the idolatry of the mind. It is thinking of the God you want and then worshiping what you think God should be. If I wanted to worship a God that was not God, I would worship a buzzard or something else, like they do in some countries of the world, and be honest about it, instead of trying to reach up and pull the mighty God down to my own cheap perception of Him.

I think the schools ought to do something about it. I think the pulpits ought to do something about it. I think publishers ought to do something about it. I think our hymn writers ought to do something about it. Our musicians ought to do something about it. We ought to get out of the wallow and look away to the stars, and walk out and listen for the awesome sweet voice that charmed Isaiah and David and all the saints down through the years.

Praise, My Soul, the King of Heaven

Praise, my soul, the King of heaven;

To His feet thy tribute bring.

Ransomed, healed, restored, forgiven,

Evermore His praises sing:

Alleluia! Alleluia!

Praise the everlasting King.

Praise Him for grace and favor

To our fathers in distress.

Praise Him still the same as ever,

Slow to chide, and swift to bless.

Alleluia! Alleluia!

Glorious in His faithfulness.

Featherlike, God tends and spares us;
Well our feeble frame He knows.
Mother like, God gently bears us,
Rescues us from all our foes.
Alleluia! Alleluia!
Widely yet His mercy flows.

Angels, help us to adore Him;
Ye behold Him face to face;
Sun and moon, bow down before Him,
Dwellers all in time and space.
Alleluia! Alleluia!
Praise with us the God of grace.
Henry F. Lyte
(1793–1847)

Chapter 9

Our Perception of God Determines Our Fellowship with God

My heart, O God, is drawn in ways beyond my comprehension. The more I know Thee, the more I love Thee; and the more I love Thee, the more I desire Thee. Create in me a pure heart, and make my heart the dwelling place of Thy presence; and let me never drift away from that aspect of my fellowship with Thee. Draw me nearer, O God; draw me nearer to Thyself in the perfection of Thy revelation. Amen.

As I begin to understand the perfection of God and how He manifests it in my life, it brings me to the point of experiencing the manifest presence of God. This is the basis of my fellowship with God. God's presence is all around us, but it is the manifest presence of God, that mysterium tremendum, that is the basis of my fellowship with Him.

"Search me, O God," David the psalmist wrote, "and know my heart: try me, and know my thoughts: and see if there be any wicked way in me, and lead me in the way everlasting" (Psalm 139:23–24). Whatever the cause, David wanted to be led by God "in the way everlasting." In order to do that, some major changes had to take place in the heart of David, and David was willing to make those changes.

In the previous chapter, I talked about hell. Hell, basically, is for those who are unlike God. Moral dissimilarity creates hell, a moral dissimilarity to God. It is the supreme purpose of God to bring us into alignment with His character. After all, we were created in the image of God, and whatever that means, there is something in us that relates to something in God, and our fellowship depends upon discovering that "something."

Whatever in my life is unlike God and contrary to the holiness of God must be eliminated from my life. That is why David said, "Search me, O God, and know my heart." David understood that he could not know his own heart, and if he could not know his own heart, how much less can people like you and me? This is the work of God and must be unhindered by our lack of knowledge of what God is doing. The person who needs to know everything and understand everything will prohibit God from doing what only God can do.

Where does our fellowship with God begin? That question needs to be answered. It is all boiled down into one theological word: reconciliation. Because of our being out of sorts with God, we need to be reconciled with God on His terms.

We do not set the terms for this reconciliation. Many people like to set their own terms, hoping that God will meet them halfway. The problem is God will never meet us halfway. It is God's way or no way. And God's way is personified for us in the Lord Jesus Christ. Our reconciliation through Jesus Christ is based upon three acts. These are acts that God has laid down to bring us into full reconciliation with Him.

Atonement is the first act. This was what Jesus Christ did on the cross for us. It was a work that only He could do, and the work that He did for us. Atonement was fully made there on the cross when Jesus died for us.

The second act would be justification. Again, Jesus Christ accomplished this on the cross. Some look at this as the legal aspect of our atonement. Jesus brought to us a finished work fully acceptable to God. Our responsibility is to accept it for ourselves.

The last act would be regeneration. This is where we come into the picture. All that Jesus Christ did on the cross would have been of no use, no value, unless it had an impact upon man's nature. What Jesus Christ did on the cross, which brought about our regeneration, was the only thing that could bring us back into full fellowship with God. This regeneration brings into us the divine nature.

The only thing that God can accept in us is His Son. And through the work of reconciliation, God has brought man to that point where he can have fellowship with God. Apart from this work, fellowship with God is not possible. God will not accept anything less than what He has set forth for us. This reconciliation brings us into conformity with the nature of God so that we can have fellowship with God and He with us.

Often in a prayer meeting, someone will pray for God to "come near to us." So many Christians have a serious problem along this line, believing that God is far away. Somehow, through some kind of means, they think we need to get God's attention and draw Him to us. If we pray long enough, if we get enough people to pray, then we entice God to draw near to us.

This is to misunderstand the whole concept of the nearness of God. God is as close to you right now as He ever was and ever will be. This is, of course, one of the attributes of God, omnipresence, which simply means that God is present everywhere. There is no place where God is not. God is as close to one thing as He is to another. And this is something hard for us to comprehend. We are trying to understand God and His attributes through our limited abilities. God has no limitation whatsoever about anything.

Keep in mind that no matter where you are or what you are doing, God is near. He does not have to be enticed or bribed to come near to us. He is already closer than we could ever imagine.

This problem of God's nearness is especially true for those Christians who have a sense of what I will call "divine remoteness." Somehow, they do not believe that God is where they are. Somehow or other, God is far removed from where they are. Because they cannot feel the connection with God, they do not believe God is near. Therefore, they have to yell and scream and try to get God's attention, as though He were off somewhere doing something else. For many who call themselves Christians, a sense of emptiness in their hearts dominates.

With Elijah in the Old Testament, it was only after all the other noise had spent itself that he was able to hear that still, small, most mighty voice of God speaking to him. Our trouble today is we cannot get still enough to hear that still, small voice.

In order to have fellowship with this God, that fellowship has to be on His terms and not ours. God has already outlined the terms of fellowship with Him, and none of these terms is negotiable. He is the One who puts down the principles for this fellowship, not us. How many Christians are attempting to keep up a relationship with God that is not actually established upon the character and nature of God? For some reason, they have taken the relationships that they have one with another and projected it onto God. This will never do.

My relationship and fellowship with another brother or sister in the Lord depend upon my physically being there. It depends upon my actually seeing them and their seeing me, and my hearing them talk and their hearing me talk. When they are not around, I do not know what they are saying, and they do not know what I am saying. In some ways, we have projected this onto God. If we cannot see God, then God cannot see us. If we cannot feel Him here, then He is not here. And if He is not here, then He does not know or understand what my situation is. How many times have we tried to explain to God the difficulties we are in and how He can help us out?

How frustrating it is to try to get hold of God, and nothing seems to work. My prayer life seems to be empty. The heavens seem to have a brass ceiling nothing can penetrate. This describes many Christians today whose perception of God is not really based upon what God has revealed to us about himself.

We have based our Christianity upon a misunderstanding of Bible truth. We have head knowledge, but no heart knowledge, of what Christianity is all about. We can explain Christianity, but we are not able to live it from our hearts. The difference between head knowledge and heart knowledge is that the heart can actually experience God, the presence of God, while the head cannot.

As I think about this subject, one question begs asking: How many Christians really have experienced God? How many have gotten beyond simply believing that God exists and experienced the presence of God? It is one thing to know about God, but it is another thing to know God in personal experience. The great delight of our Father, which art in heaven, is for us to experience Him in a way that He deserves.

I am rather passionate about reading the Bible. I firmly believe in the importance of spending time alone with God in the written Word, and I encourage others to spend as much time in the Word of God as possible. I have discovered that when I spend time in the Word of God, I will experience the Living Word. If I have not experienced the Living Word, I have not really read the Bible. The Bible is not a textbook so I can answer questions on a quiz somewhere. The Bible cannot be compared to any other book in the world. When I come to the Bible, and when I spend time reading and meditating upon the Scriptures, I am entering a world where God is dominant and desires to reveal himself to the worshiping heart.

As I get into the Word of God, it begins to reveal God to me. And as that divine illumination takes place under the guidance of the Holy Spirit, I then begin to see God for who He really is—not some caricature somebody has drawn to explain God to me. The great secret of the Christian life is to begin experiencing God as He desires me to experience Him. God's greatest delight is to bring me into His presence.

I am afraid that for all practical purposes, we have only theological Christians in the church today, not deeply spiritual Christians. We have wonderful head knowledge of the Bible and can give "a reason to everyone who asks us about the hope within us," but it does not go further than that.

As I get to know God, I begin to experience aspects of God that whet my appetite for more of God. I can never have enough of God. A growing yearning to be near God begins to develop, and I begin to recognize that God is within me; and I want to experience this God who is within me. I yearn for a manifestation of the presence of God, a degree of fellowship with Him that goes beyond mere head knowledge. This is not something we can explain. If we could explain it to everybody's satisfaction, it would not be God. God is much more than we can explain or boil down to human understanding. God can be experienced only in the heart, which creates the atmosphere of praise and worship and adoration.

The prevailing condition among Christians today, as I see it, is that there is a sense of God's absence among us. Many believe in God. Many worship God and even sing about Him. But it is almost as if He is not there. This has brought Christianity down below any other religion in the world. Believe me when I say that Christianity is not like any other religion. Christianity begins with God and envelops the human heart that has been redeemed and comes back once again to the heart of God.

The apostle Paul makes this clear when he writes:

If ye then be risen with Christ, seek those things which are above, where Christ sitteth on the right hand of God. Set your affection on things above, not on things on the earth. For ye are dead, and your life is hid with Christ in God.

Colossians 3:1–3

This is the posture of the Christian. We are seeking those things that are above. We are not being hindered by the world around us, but we are setting our affections on things above. We are looking up for our redemption, which is in Jesus Christ.

The reality of Jesus Christ is the basis of our daily fellowship with God. If we just acknowledge that there is a God somewhere and that Jesus Christ died for our sins and that one day when we die, we are going to go to heaven, we have not really grasped the dynamics of fellowship with God.

My fellowship with God is much more than "one day I am going to die and go to heaven." My fellowship with God is experiencing the manifest presence of God in my day-to-day living—not just a Sunday morning experience that cannot be replicated throughout the week. The dynamics of our worship is an everyday experience, or it is not true worship and we do not understand who God really is.

As our fellowship with God grows day by day, the Holy Spirit unfolds to us the reality of the Christian life. The qualities of Jesus Christ are becoming our qualities. What He is, we are becoming. I am not talking about His deity. I am talking about the holiness of His perfection. Jesus Christ did not die on the cross merely so that one day we can go to heaven, which certainly is our hope; it is much deeper than that.

Jesus died on the cross, rose from the dead on the third day, ascended into heaven, and sent the Holy Spirit on the Day of Pentecost to give us His character and His nature to be a testimony to the world around us. Our testimony is not that we have cleaned up our life. Any religion can do that. Our testimony is that we are like Christ, and people around us will begin to experience Jesus Christ as they begin to understand us.

Now, what are those qualities of Jesus? As we peruse the Scriptures, these qualities of His perfection are unveiled to us. These qualities include holiness, unselfishness, love, kindness, forgiveness, zeal, humility, and heavenly-mindedness. As we study the life of Jesus, we begin to see these qualities, and that these qualities are part of our Christian experience. Day by day, I am becoming more Christ like in my life.

The more like Jesus Christ I become, the more intimate is my fellowship with Him. Those things in my life that are contrary to Him need to be crucified and put out of my life so that I may go on in the fullness of spiritual perfection.

A great many are disconcerted about the term spiritual perfection. They make excuses for themselves, saying that nobody is perfect. But there is Someone who is perfect. That perfect One is Jesus Christ. As we pursue Him in daily fellowship and in the perfection of His character and nature, we begin to become more and more like Him. The more we become like Him, the more our fellowship with Him takes on the reality that Jesus Christ desires in all of us.

Out in the world we cannot find anything that will help us in our fellowship with God. We must decisively turn our backs on the world and walk in the shadow of the cross. Whatever it costs us is worth the fellowship we enjoy this side of glory.

Draw Me Nearer

I am Thine, O Lord, I have heard Thy voice,

And it told Thy love to me;

But I long to rise in the arms of faith

And be closer drawn to Thee.

Refrain:

Draw me nearer, nearer blessed Lord,

To the cross where Thou hast died;

Draw me nearer, nearer, nearer blessed Lord,

To Thy precious, bleeding side.

Consecrate me now to Thy service, Lord,

By the pow'r of grace divine;

Let my soul look up with a steadfast hope,

And my will be lost in Thine.

Oh, the pure delight of a single hour

That before Thy throne I spend,

When I kneel in prayer, and with Thee, my God,

I commune as friend with friend!

There are depths of love that I cannot know

Till I cross the narrow sea;

There are heights of joy that I may not reach

Till I rest in peace with Thee.

Frances J. Crosby

(1820–1915)

Chapter 10

Our Perception of God's Perfection

I long for Thee, O God, in all Thy perfection. My mind cannot comprehend the wonders of Thy perfection, and I stagger trying to understand Thee. What my mind cannot grasp, my heart can in full wonder and adoration. Fill my heart with Thyself. The heaven and heaven of heavens cannot contain Thee; how much less this mind of mine. Amen.

The challenge before me is to describe that which cannot be described. When describing God, who is unlimited in every aspect, we are challenged by our human limitations. God makes the greatest demand on our intelligence and imagination and powers of reason, requiring us to picture a mode of being we are not familiar with, a mode of being wholly beyond ourselves, a mode of being unlike anything we have ever known.

We must keep in mind one thing: All I say about God is still not God, because theology, at its finest moment, can do no more than tell us about God. To know about God and to know God are two absolutely different things. Most people confuse knowing about God with knowing God, and this, in my opinion, is at the core of many of our problems in the evangelical church today.

Let me say that if you ever know God, you are going to have to enter in by the new birth, by the illumination of the Holy Spirit, and by the revelation of the Spirit. There must be revelation and illumination. You have to have truth revealed to you, but until there is illumination of that truth, it does not do you any good. Only the Holy Spirit can make us know God. That is why when we speak of the Holy Spirit, we ought not to speak apologetically, and nobody ought to be ashamed to preach about the Holy Spirit or be afraid to talk about Him, for the reason that only He can make us know.

Theology can teach us about God, and that is what this book is all about.

One problem in describing God is that we use ourselves as a pattern, push that up into the heavens, and say that is what God is like. God is bigger than we are, of course. But He is one size and we are another size, so we begin to think of God in terms of our limitations. When we try to describe God this way, we end up with a caricature of God, a God that is not worthy of our worship. Too many people are worshiping the God of their own imaginations.

If we are really going to understand God, we need to see Him in light of infinity. I mean by that, God is infinite in every aspect of himself. What I mean about the infinitude of God is that God knows no limit, and right there is where we stop. The human mind can go a long way, but it cannot go all the way to limitlessness. But God is limitless, boundless, and has no end. This defies every definition we could ever come up with. There is no end to anything in God, and He has no bounds.

The vast ocean has a boundary, but God has no boundary. Whatever God is, He is without limit or bounds, and whatever God has, He has without limit or measure. These are words that can be used only about something created, and God is the Uncreated One.

When we come to describe God, we sometimes use words carelessly. We often say that something is unlimited. A company's wealth is unlimited, an athlete has unlimited energy, an artist takes unlimited pains to do his painting. The danger of taking the word unlimited and pulling it down into our sphere is that we then associate God and His unlimitedness with our understanding of unlimited.

Take the word measureless, for example. Measureless is a word we can use only of God. Anytime you have some kind of measurement, it has to do with created things giving an account of themselves. But it cannot be applied to God.

In our description of God, we cannot use imperfections, because God does not have limitations or imperfections of any sort. God is in a category all by himself. Everything we describe by limitations is contingent and relative, whereas God is self-existent, an absolute. Therefore, He is a boundless ocean; and none can bound Him, and none can fathom Him, and none can describe how far out He goes in infinite distance in all that He is.

Measure applies to created things and can never be associated with God. We have liquid measurements and measurements of energy and sound measurements. We have measures of light. We say a bulb is so many watts, and we have numbers for pluralities: ones, twos, fives, and some tens. We can even measure intelligence. We measure our brain and our ability to do things, but when we do that, we are imperfect, small, and limited—not infinite.

God cannot be measured and cannot be weighed, for He is not composed of matter. You cannot figure God in distance, for God fills all distance. You cannot measure God, for God has no extension in space. You cannot measure the energy of God or the sound God makes or the light He gives off, or anything else in their absolute pluralities. God is one—one God, we praise Thee.

None of these words or concepts can touch God or describe Him. They describe only imperfect things that God has made, not God himself. They are the way we see the work of God's hands. It is His fingerprint in creation.

Look on the work of God's hands and you will see it. You see a mountain or a man and you have size there. Size is a relative thing. A man weighing two hundred pounds is nothing compared to a mountain.

But with God, there are no sizes, no degrees, no measurements, and no pluralities, because God is just God.

Frederick Faber once wrote a hymn about the infinity of God ("The Greatness of God"). Nobody ever sings it, but he wrote it and got it out of his system. I have read it and it has blessed me.

O Majesty unspeakable and dread!

Wert Thou less mighty than Thou art,

Thou wert, O Lord! too great for our belief,

Too little for our heart.

I hear people say, "We have a big God." I really do not like that, because I do not think we ought to pull God down to our level. I think God is too holy, too infinite, too high, too wonderful, too glorious to even think of Him like that.

If God were just a big God, He would be so big He would scare us, but He would be too little for us to worship. I could not worship a God who was just an oversized man. I could not even worship a God who was a huge man. If God were simply a huge man, then I could say, "He's bigger than I am, but here I am."

This great God is infinite, and so I have no greatness apart from God.

But greatness, which is infinite makes room

For all things in its lap to lie;

We should be crushed by a magnificence

Short of infinity.

We share in what is infinite: 'tis ours,

For we and it alike are Thine;

What I enjoy, great God! by right of Thee

Is more than doubly mine.

Thus doth Thy grandeur make us grand ourselves;

'Tis goodness bids us fear;

Thy greatness makes us brave as children are,

When those they love are near.

Frederick Faber

(1814–1863)

God is infinite, and because God is infinite, you and I can be bold and brave in the universe, just the same as the little boy who is brave when his father is around.

How could I stand myself if I did not believe in the infinite God? How could I endure myself if I did not know that God is eternal? How could I endure the passing of my years if I did not know that I had been baptized into the heart of the One who knows no years, who is the Ancient of Days, who had no beginning and can have no end? How could I accept my weakness if I did not know that I had been baptized into the heart of the One who has infinite strength? So this is our God, and this is the God we adore.

God is what He is without limit. He knows no extent, He knows no measure, and if there is a point where God is not, it would mean that God is not really who He says He is.

There is a limit to great countries and a limit to great wealth, but there is no place where you can put a boundary and say, "God, do not overflow this." God speaks to the sea, and says, "This far, and no farther." But who can speak to God and say, "This far and no farther"? Who dares tell God what He can do or cannot do?

If you are thinking of a limit, you are not thinking about God. But if you think and think and think, out and out, and up and up, and try to think as far out as God and then you break down—do not let it worry you. Saint Augustine had his troubles with it. So did Paul and David and Isaiah. No human being can think infinitude. Nobody can think it; you must believe it. You must believe it in your heart.

I cannot take you by the hand and lead you into the kingdom of God. I can only point you to the Lamb of God, and then it is between God and you. In the same way, I cannot by any means describe the infinitude of God. I can only point with wonder, amazement, and awestruck admiration and say, "Behold God." After that, it is you and God.

What does all this mean to us? If God is infinite—and all theologians believe this, the Bible teaches it, and we sing about it—what does it mean to us now? Is it simply a lesson in theology that will be examined one day? No, not that. If this is true—and it is true—then certain things about God are true.

If God is infinite, then His love is infinite. There is a love closer than the love of a mother, and that is the love of God. A mother's love goes so far, but there is a limit to it. A mother can die and her love dies with her; but God cannot die, and because He cannot die, His love never dies.

Right here someone will say, "Did not Jesus die, and do we not sing, 'When Christ the mighty Maker died, for man the creature's sin'?"

Yes. The second person of the Trinity took upon himself the form of a man and died for our sins, but the eternal God remained alive and raised Him from the dead. Deity never died, but the man called Jesus, who was both God and man, died for our sins. No contradiction there. No confusion at all. God cannot die. God is the immortal who has only immortality dwelling in light, which no man can approach. So the love of God is infinite. You can be certain of this.

Love of people is not infinite. It is an awful thing to fall in love and then fall back out of love. I always think how shocking it is when in a divorce situation a person will say, "I no longer love him." She once did, but no longer. Love did not last.

We sometimes hear about mothers who forsake their children, so even the finest love that the world knows can fail. The love of a father, mother, sister, or wife has limits; but the love of God has none because God is infinite, and anything God has is limitless. There is one thing you can be sure about: There is no limit to the love of God.

Some believe in the complete salvation of the universe. They believe that when Christ died, He died for everyone, including the devil and demons. That is universalism, which I do not go along with. But as far as the love of God is concerned, the love of God is infinite enough to take in all of heaven and hell too. God, in His infinite planning, planned that only those who repent and believe shall be saved.

For the love of God is broader

Than the measure of our mind;

And the heart of the Eternal

Is most wonderfully kind.

Frederick W. Faber

(1814–1863)

Recently I was praying and thinking about how vast the grace of God is compared with our human sin. It is a peculiar contradiction. For example, if you do not think your sin is big, then the Lord cannot save you. If you think your sin is bigger than God, then He cannot save you. You have to realize that to you, your sin is big; but God is infinite, and therefore God is bigger than all your sin. Where sin abounds, the grace of God does much more abound. When God says "more," referring to himself, we must extend our imagination into borderline infinity. When God says "much more" and puts a qualifying word behind it, what can you do but kneel and say, "My Lord and my God, how grace does much more abound"?

When you have for your medicine that which has no limit to cure a disease, which has a limit, you can be sure the patient is going to get well. When the infinite, limitless grace of God attacks the finite limit of sin in a man, that sin has no chance. If we will only repent and turn from it, God will pulverize it and whirl it into immensity, where it can never be known again while eternity rolls on eternity.

That is what happened to my sin. That is what happens to the sin of everyone who believes.

I am not making a fuss with the devil; I will let God handle him. God is the only one who can. But I would like, in a sneaky way, to have the devil know that Jesus Christ our Lord is infinite, and His blood is infinite, and the purchase of His blood is infinite; and if all the sands of the seashore and all the stars in the sky were human beings, and if every corpuscle in the bloodstream of every human being in the world was a human being, and they had all sinned as bad as Judas did, still the grace of God, being infinite and limitless, would have no limit. As Nicolaus Ludwig von Zinzendorf expressed:

Lord, I believe, were sinners more

Than sands upon the ocean shore,

For all Thou hast the ransom given,

Purchased for all peace, life, and heaven.

God could send a team of angels to count my sins, and in ten years or so, they could have them all added up and say, "Here's the total," and it would string clear across the room. The angel might say, "I guess he is doomed." But God would say, "No, look at My grace. It extends, not across the room, but from eternity past to eternity to come." We sing of the infinite grace of our loving God, and it is proper and correct that we should.

This concept of infinitude also applies to the atonement, when Christ died for us.

When Jesus Christ died on the cross, it was enough. Personally, I am glad to have enough of something. When Jesus died on the cross, it took Him only six hours. But because it was infinity dying, the man who died was the Deity who could not die. But because God counted the infinity there, to Him it was enough.

I believe Jesus died for everyone, and when He died on the cross, He not only died for the elect, but He died for every human being who was ever born in the world or ever will be born. I believe He died for every baby who died at birth and for every man and woman who lived to be one hundred or more. I believe He died for all.

We can go around the world telling people that Jesus Christ died for them.

No man who has ever lived has been too much of a sinner to go beyond the infinite atonement of Jesus Christ. If every man were a sinner as bad as Judas Iscariot, the atonement of Jesus Christ would still cover him. If someone had only told Judas and he had repented, there might have been a Saint Judas today.

Another description we have in this regard has to do with the patience of Jesus—the infinite patience of Jesus, the patience of God, with the power to save. He has infinite power to save and breaks the power of canceled sin. Paul Rader used to say, "You name it, and God will break it." He was so right.

Jesus, Thy Blood and Righteousness

Lord, I believe, were sinners more
Than sands upon the ocean shore,
For all Thou hast the ransom given,
Purchased for all peace, life, and heaven.

Lord, I believe the price is paid
For every soul, the atonement made;
And every soul Thy grace may prove,
Loved with an everlasting love.

Jesus, be endless praise to Thee,
Whose boundless mercy hath for me,
For me, and all Thine hands have made,
An everlasting ransom paid.

Ah, give to all Thy servants, Lord,
With power to speak Thy quickening Word,
That sinners to Thy wounds may flee,
And find eternal life in Thee.

Thou God of power, Thou God of love,
Let the whole world Thy mercy prove;
Now let Thy Word o'er all prevail;
Now take the spoils of death and hell.
Nicolaus Ludwig von Zinzendorf
(1700–1760)

Chapter 11
Our Perception of God's Grace

Our Father, our hearts hunger for the fullness of Thy nature. We do not deserve to be in Thy presence, but Thou hast made it possible for us to come boldly to the throne of grace. That grace is wonderful in us. Although I may not fully comprehend Thy grace, I can benefit from it today. Amen.

One compromised aspect of God has to do with His grace. If our perception of God is compromised, everything about our understanding of God is also compromised. I think this matter of grace is one of the most important perceptions of God to fall under this category of misconception.

If we do not understand God, we will never understand His grace and its full impact on our lives. This is reflected in our hymnology. I have a collection of hymnals, and whenever I am visiting somewhere, I like to look through their hymnal. Recently I looked through a rather modern hymnal and found the hymn "Amazing Grace," written by John Newton. Whenever we think of grace, this hymn always comes to mind. I noticed in this hymnal that they had made a significant change. I certainly am not a fan of those who try to change a hymn in order to satisfy their own taste.

The first line of this hymn goes, "Amazing grace, how sweet the sound, that saved a wretch like me!" This is the familiar version of that hymn. However, in this modern, up-to-date hymnal, the first line was changed: "Amazing grace, how sweet the sound, that saved a one like me." Quite a significant change, in my opinion.

Some people tend not to quite grasp the idea that we are, or were at one time, a wretch. It simply does not go down very easily. We are willing to say that we are not perfect, that we missed the mark, or that we are not really up to par. But we are not ready to say that in ourselves we are nothing more than a wretch.

Until we come to that point of understanding what wretches we are, we will never understand the amazing grace of God. It takes a wretch like me to experience the amazing grace of God. Some people believe that God's grace enables Him to put up with certain conditions that are not quite up to His standard. We have a different discernment of what grace is all about.

Our British friends talk about the "gracious queen." Or we might see a man who is very sympathetic, long-suffering, and generous, and we might look at him and say, "There's a very gracious man."

The problem is that we define grace from our standpoint. We believe the grace of God is that He tolerates sin because He loves us so much. That is the price of His love for us. This, however, is far from what the Bible teaches. God's grace is not something that we can use to manipulate God into some corner and get Him to do something we want Him to do against His will. God cannot be manipulated.

When we explore the concept of God's grace, we cannot separate it from His other attributes. God does not lay aside one attribute in order to pick up another attribute. In God, there is a complete sense of oneness. He is not like my watch that is put together, and all the parts synchronize and work together harmoniously. God's grace is in complete conformity to every other attribute of God.

To understand this, I need to say that it is out of the goodness of God that grace comes. Mercy, as I have stated before, is God's goodness confronting human guilt, and grace is God's goodness confronting human demerit.

Prior to man's fall in the garden of Eden, God's grace was not evident. Not that it was not there—it was just that there was no situation that brought that aspect of God's character to light. Once man fell into the cesspool of sin and became polluted, God's grace came out like a shining contrast. Paul writes about this in Romans 5:20: "But where sin abounded, grace did much more abound." Grace, like all God's attributes, carries with it the "much more" aspect.

God was always gracious. He never has been less gracious than He is now, and He never will be more gracious than He is now. But until sin came into the world, God's grace was not evident. Now we can see this aspect of God, particularly in our own lives, when we realize what wretches we are in comparison to the holiness of God.

Allow me to lay out some facts about grace that should encourage our hearts.

First, grace is God's good pleasure.

Grace brings into favor one that has previously been in disfavor. It is the unchangeable grace of God, and it never ceases to be what it is. Throughout the Scriptures, grace and favor are interchangeable words. You will find the word favor occurring and you will find the word grace occurring, but if you look at it in the original languages, you will find they are the same word as originally given but translated favor or grace, apparently at the whim of the translator.

Although there is three times as much material in the New Testament about grace as there is in the Old Testament, there is four times as much about mercy in the Old Testament as there is in the New. It is virtually impossible to separate God's grace from either the Old Testament or the New Testament. It permeates everything that has to do with God's interaction with mankind.

The second fact about grace is that Christ is the only channel through which grace flows.

The Scriptures clearly declare, "For the law was given by Moses, but grace and truth came by Jesus Christ" (John 1:17). Here we need to be careful that we do not misread this and find ourselves in a dismal swamp of misunderstanding. Some people have taken this to mean that because it says the law was given by Moses but grace came by Jesus Christ, Moses knew only the law and Christ knows only grace.

This is to completely misunderstand grace. Grace was in the time of Moses, and the law was in the time of Christ. The Bible clearly declares that Christ came, born of a woman, born under the law. In the Old Testament, it says that Noah found grace in the eyes of the Lord. Grace operated after the Ten Commandments were given, and grace operated before the Ten Commandments were given. Grace was operative back in the sixth chapter of Genesis, and grace has been operating ever since. There is no ebb and flow of God's grace. It is a steady stream.

How can it be otherwise? God must always act like himself and can never contradict any of His attributes.

When Scripture says that the law was given by Moses and grace and truth came by Jesus Christ, it did not mean that it came when Jesus was born in Bethlehem, because there is an awful lot said about grace before Jesus was born. If the baby Jesus and Christ Jesus and the dying Lamb and the risen Lamb had brought grace into the world, then there would have been no grace before Mary's baby was born in the manger in Bethlehem. Grace operated from the early days, and grace prevented God from slaying Adam and Eve when they sinned. Noah found grace in God's sight, and it was grace that saved the eight people from the flood. It was grace from the very beginning, all down through the years. Grace had no beginning, and it has no end.

So grace came by Jesus Christ, but grace did not come when Christ was born in Bethlehem. Grace had been in Jesus Christ from the beginning of the world. Christ was slain before the foundation of the world, as the Scriptures set forth for us, before the world was hurled into its orbit and populated by man. Grace had been in Jesus Christ and always was so.

Grace could not come by Moses because Moses was a sinner. Grace could not come by Abraham, for Abraham was a sinner. Grace could not come by David, for David was a sinner, a happy singing sinner, but a sinner nevertheless, and he needed grace himself. God could not send grace through any of them. Grace could not come by Paul. Sometimes people almost make a god or a demigod out of the man Paul. He would be the last one in the world to allow this, and he objected to it whenever it came up. Grace comes by Jesus Christ—always has and always will—and there is never any grace apart from Jesus Christ.

I should also include here what I will refer to as governmental grace.

This is grace that prevents God from destroying sinful men and women when they boast. The fact that sinful people can boast of their sin and continue in it is a demonstration of God's grace. If God's grace were not operative, that man or woman would be struck dead in their tracks. God's grace prevented Him from slaying the heinous and brutal dictators down through the years who were responsible for murdering millions of people. Sometimes we do not think of grace in this fashion.

If God did not operate by this governmental grace, very few people would be alive today. This grace saves countries like the United States from destruction. In that sense, the grace is for everybody, and everybody profits by the grace of God. That is a demonstration of the good favor of God, the kindness of God, the goodness of God, the long-suffering of God. Let me quickly point out this is not saving grace. This grace keeps God from destroying the sinner.

Then, of course, there is saving grace.

Saving grace is another matter, and it is a narrower matter and comes to us only through Jesus Christ. God's grace keeps Him from destroying people, but on the other hand, the saving grace of God brings people into fellowship with Him. This is the grace we think of—the amazing grace of God that saves a wretch like me.

Grace is also the kindness of God's heart.

As a young person, I used to hear people say about a person that he was a kindhearted man. Well, God is a kindhearted God. He is a God of goodwill and cordiality and is that way all through. God is what He is all the time, all the way through without any upsurge or down surge.

You can look at God from any direction; He is always the same, and He is the same all the way through, always, toward all people, forever. You will never run into any meanness in God or resentment or ill will. God never fluctuates in His feelings as man fluctuates. We can be good-hearted one day and the next day mean as a cat. Not so with God.

Through the years, I have met good Christians, and they go to heaven by the same grace that gets me to heaven. I have noticed they were all right as long as everything was going their way. They seemed to be very good and cordial, and then they shocked me by pouting. They were not all the same, all the way through, all the time. There was resentfulness, ill will, but there is none of this in God.

God has no present ill will toward anybody anywhere in the universe. No one can "get under God's skin," as we say about ourselves. We can put up with somebody for only so long, but then they get under our skin. This is not in the character of God at all.

Just as the holiness of God requires that heaven be empty of all iniquity, those who are iniquitous do not receive the favor of God through Jesus Christ. They must be cast out finally because they cannot be permitted to pollute heaven with their unholy presence. God will never allow anybody to compromise His holiness, and God's grace goes on to affect each situation.

One final fact about grace is that God's grace is infinite.

Everything God has and is, is infinite. Infinite means "boundless, without end." This is hard to grasp for us who are so limited in what we do. God has no beginning and no end, and nothing in God has been created. We, who have been created, cannot fully comprehend the nature of uncreated.

I believe in God's boundlessness and that there is no border anywhere in God. For man, it is a simple matter of going out and floating around the earth and coming down again on our rockets. It is a nice engineering feat, and nice work if you can get it and do something adventurous and all that. But it does not shake my belief in the great God Almighty. You can get in that same little rocket, ride out until the stars are burned out, and still you have not reached the boundaries of God Almighty. God contains all space and all matter and all creation.

The Bible talks about God sitting on the circle of the earth: "It is he that sitteth upon the circle of the earth, and the inhabitants thereof are as grasshoppers; that stretcheth out the heavens as a curtain, and spreadeth them out as a tent to dwell in" (Isaiah 40:22). All creation is but dust in the balance and nothing before God.

Simply try to compare God's grace with our needs. No matter what our need is, it does not measure against the amazing grace of God. God was always a gracious God, but until sin came into the world, it was never manifested and nobody knew it.

As we meditate on God's grace, we are affected by the overwhelming plenitude of goodness and kindness on the part of God. If every mosquito in all the swamplands of the world were a sinner, every star in heaven a sinner, and every grain of sand by the seashore a sinner, the grace of God could swallow it all without effort, for where sin abounds, grace doth much more abound.

Philosophically, theologically, practically, and experientially, I am a believer in the grace of God. My life is a testimony of God's amazing grace. God's goodness and faithfulness are demonstrated in everyone's life. The worse off you are, the more the favor of God will shine in your life.

Amazing Grace

Amazing grace! How sweet the sound
That saved a wretch like me!
I once was lost, but now am found;
Was blind, but now, I see.

'Twas grace that taught my heart to fear,
And grace my fears relieved;
How precious did that grace appear,
The hour I first believed!

Through many dangers, toils and snares,
I have already come;
'Tis grace hath brought me safe thus far,
And grace will lead me home.

The Lord has promised good to me,
His word my hope secures;
He will my shield and portion be,
As long as life endures.

And when this flesh and heart shall fail,
And mortal life shall cease;
I shall possess within the veil
A life of joy and peace.

When we've been there ten thousand years,
Bright shining as the sun,
We've no less days to sing God's praise

Than when we'd first begun.

John Newton

1725–1807)

Chapter 12
Our Perception of God's Mercy

O Lord, Thou knowest that we are not worthy to come before Thy presence, before the mystery of which angels stand in wonder. Deal with us, not according to our deserts, but according to Thy infinite mercy, by the Holy Spirit, for Christ's sake. Amen.

The Scriptures abound with the truth that God is a merciful God. Mercy is something that God is; it is a facet of His unitary being. As a diamond has many facets, so does God with regard to His attributes. God is one, and one facet of God's character is mercy.

Both the Old and New Testaments declare the mercy of God. Sometimes we think there is more of God's mercy in the New Testament. The odd thing is the Old Testament has more than four times as much to say about mercy as the New Testament—that is, it is odd seen against a background of error, which we have been taught most of our lives. We have been taught that the Old Testament is a book of law, and the New Testament a book of grace. The Old Testament is a book of judgment, and the New Testament a book of mercy. If the God of the Old Testament is a God of thunder and judgment, in the New Testament He is a God of meekness and mercy. But the truth is, God is merciful and God's mercy is perfect. His mercy is infinitely perfect.

It is impossible to separate the Old Testament from the New Testament. It takes the whole Bible to make the Word of God. Trying to isolate one part of the Bible from another part is to do great damage to the Word of God. Trying to separate law from grace is a very dangerous thing and usually leads to heresy. There can be no law without grace, and no grace without law.

God's infinite goodness is that God desires His creatures' happiness. That desire in God, which has an irresistible urge to bestow blessedness, takes no pleasure in the death of the wicked but does take pleasure in the pleasure of His people. God suffers along with His friends and grieves over His foes. It is that in God which we call mercy that looks with compassion upon men and women who deserve judgment.

Mercy, according to the Old Testament meaning, is to stoop in kindness to an inferior. It is to have pity upon another and to be actively compassionate. I deliberately use the words active and actively, for I do not like the words passive and passivity and various forms of the word passive. The mercy of God is not a passive thing, but active. God is compassionate, but He is actively compassionate.

Grieving over the sins of the world is not going to help the world very much. God is not that kind of a God. His mercy is active, not passive. He has pity upon mankind, but it is active pity. He stops in kindness to His inferiors.

We must be careful to understand that none of God's attributes spring out of the need of man. All God's attributes reveal His character in and of himself. Man, on the other hand, benefits from those attributes, and the great challenge of our lives is to connect with those attributes. The only way we can do that is through Jesus Christ.

Let me lay out a few truths concerning the mercy of God.

First of all, the mercy of God never had a beginning.

If you were to go down to the Mississippi River, you would see a river so wide you could not cross it without getting into a boat and paddling. If you wanted to find the source, you would have to keep on paddling north until you got to a place where the river became a stream, where you could toss a pebble across, and where a cow could wade in and drink, way up in northern Minnesota. The Mississippi River has her beginnings there. The great broad river of the Mississippi has a source.

Never must we think of God's mercy as being like that river, originating somewhere and then flowing out. It never began to be because it is an attribute of the uncreated God and therefore always was, and it has never been any more or less than it is now.

Sometimes we think that at one time, way back in the past, God was very wondrously merciful. He walked in the garden with Adam. He walked with Enoch, and then Enoch was no more because God took him. When we read the Bible stories of God's mercy, we say, "God must have been wonderfully merciful back there, but that was before the day of gas chambers and brutalities and all the stuff we have today. God is not as merciful anymore."

To say that is to malign the name of God. Being infinitely merciful, God never can be any more merciful than He is now and never was any more merciful in the past. The God who told Noah to build the ark and save the race of humanity is the same God with whom we have to deal today.

God will never be any less merciful than He is now, because being infinite, He cannot cease to be infinite, and being perfect, He cannot have any imperfection. So the mercy of God is what God is, because God is who He is.

God's mercy cannot be affected by anything anyone does.

So many preachers and evangelists tell tearjerker stories, wanting the stream of mercy to flow out of the human eye, thinking that if we cry and beg, God will have mercy upon us. God will have mercy upon you if your heart is as hard as stone. If you were never to weep over your iniquity, God is still a merciful God. He cannot be anything else but merciful, and though everybody in the world might turn atheist, every human being turn into a beast, and all the world turn into devils, it would not change the mercy of God in the slightest. God would still be as merciful as He is now. If Christ were to die a hundred times on the cross, it would not make God any more merciful than He is now, because God is as merciful as mercy can be. Being God, He will never be less merciful.

Nothing can increase, diminish, or alter the quality of God's mercy.

The cross did not increase the mercy of God. Let us remember we ought to be good, sound Bible readers, and we ought to have our theology right. Let us remember that the mercy of God did not begin at Calvary. The mercy of God led to Calvary. It was because God was merciful that Christ died on the cross. Christ did not die on the cross in order to make God merciful; God was already merciful, which is why Christ died. It was the mercy of God that brought Jesus to earth. And when He came down, He came down and died because He was already as merciful as it is possible to be. God is merciful and the source of all mercy, and the Father of mercies and the God of all comfort, so that nothing can make Him any more merciful than He has always been.

Let us not imagine falsely that Jesus Christ our Lord is up before the throne of an angry-faced God, pleading for His people. He is pleading all right, and He is praying there, and He is making intercession for us, but the God to whom He is making intercession is just as merciful now, no more and no less, than He was before His Son died on the cross. The cross did not make the mercy of God any more merciful, or the quality of that mercy any more perfect, or the amount of that mercy any greater. Neither does the intercession of Christ make Him more merciful.

Notice that the mercy of God operates in a certain way.

Whenever there is inequity, whenever there is immorality of any kind, the justice of God confronts it. That which is not moral is immoral. We have one sin; we call that immorality. All sin is immorality in that it is not morality. Jealousy, as well as that snide expression about somebody, is immorality. That trimming on your income tax report is immorality. Losing your temper and yelling at your husband is immorality. Everything we do that is wrong is immorality. Immorality is inequity, injustice—that which is not just, right, and level.

Judgment is God's justice confronting moral inequity, whereas mercy is God's goodness confronting human guilt and suffering.

We are all recipients of God's mercy. We think we are not, but we are. There is not an atheist in the world that is not the recipient of God's mercy right now. We have so much, and we live in such a way that if justice had its way unrestrained, without mercy, God would rain fire from the Rio Grande to the Hudson Bay. All men and women are recipients of the mercy of God, for all have sinned and come short of the glory of God, and mercy postpones the execution, for God is not willing that any should perish, but that all should come to repentance.

We need to notice one thing that distinguishes Christians from all other people and religions in the world: Mercy can cancel or pardon by the atonement when justice sees inequity. Death is a sentence meted out, but mercy brought Christ to the cross. Justice and mercy see righteousness instead of iniquity, and when the just God looks down upon a sinner who has been covered by the atoning merits of Jesus' blood, He sees not a sinner anymore, but a justified individual. That is the doctrine of justification by faith, the very foundation of redemption and one of the great cornerstones of the church today.

When we see it like this, we wonder about one thing: Since God is perfect, self-contained, and self-sufficient, how can He suffer?—for God does suffer. He sent His Son to suffer, so I can only paraphrase the language of Frederick Faber: "How Thou canst suffer, O my God, and be the God Thou art, is darkness to my intellect but sunshine to my heart."

I know that justice sentenced me to that. The soul that sinneth shall die, and I know that I should die and that hell should swallow me up. But I also know that Christ died on the cross for my sins. He went out there and in darkness did something I do not know. I am afraid of the man who is too smart about the atonement. I am afraid of the man who can explain it too well, for surely it was the mystery of godliness. Surely what He did can never enter the mind of man or be fully understood. Surely what He did that awful, dark day, when it became as dark as a thousand midnights in the Cypress Swamp, we can never explain or understand intellectually.

Peter, who thought about this as much as you and I, lived with Jesus three years and saw Him go out and die on the cross, and saw Him after He had risen from the dead, said in odd language, "Angels desire to look into these things." The very angels in heaven desire to know about this. I do not know about that atonement. I do not know what He did, but I know that whatever He did satisfied the heart of God forever. I know that whatever He did turned my iniquity into righteousness, turned my inequity into equity, and turned the sentence of death into a judgment of life. I know it did that, so I can only stand before Him and say, "How Thou canst suffer, O my God, and be the God Thou art, is darkness to my intellect but sunshine to my heart."

Do not ask your head about this. If you cannot think about it, get on your knees and say, "Thou knowest, O my Lord and my God." Maybe someday in that bright tomorrow, maybe with clearer eyes and brighter vision, we will look upon the wonder of the atonement and know what it means. Not all of the theologians who have ever lived can explain this. Together they can only stand before Him and say He gave himself, the just for the unjust, that He might bring us to God.

I do not understand the mystery of it. I know the joy and the sunshine of His effects upon me and those who know God.

The mercy of God is moral and theological doctrine to me. The mercy of God is my life and my breath. Oh the mercy of God, that God is compassionate, that He stoops to have pity and mercy upon His people. How approachable the mercy of God is, how accessible and how completely gracious God is, and how He has no pleasure in the death of anyone, particularly the wicked. He is the Father of mercies. He is very compassionate and full of tender mercy, and He is not willing that any should perish, but that all should come to repentance. This is the message we must tell the world. This is the witness we must give to the world. We need to go into the world and tell them who God really is.

We must go into the world and tell them that God is merciful and gracious, and slow to anger and full of loving-kindness, and that He sent His Son to die for their sins. There is a door open. It is the door of mercy, and it is open wide for us.

The Mercy of God is an Ocean Divine

The mercy of God is an ocean divine,

A boundless and fathomless flood;

Launch out in the deep, cut away the shoreline,

And be lost in the fullness of God.

Refrain:

Launch out, into the deep,

Oh, let the shore line go;

Launch out, launch out in the ocean divine,

Out where the full tides flow.

But many, alas! only stand on the shore,

And gaze on the ocean so wide;

They never have ventured its depths to explore,
Or to launch on the fathomless tide.

And others just venture away from the land,
And linger so near to the shore
That the surf and the slime that beat over the strand
Dash o'er them in floods evermore.

Oh, let us launch out on this ocean so broad,
Where floods of salvation o'erflow;
Oh, let us be lost in the mercy of God,
Till the depths of His fullness we know.
Albert B. Simpson
(1843–1919)

Chapter 13
Our Perception of God's Goodness

Out of Thy goodness, O God, Thou has reached down and blessed me beyond my comprehension. My praise to Thee, O God, fills my heart with joy in expectation of good things from Thee. May my life be a testimony of Thy goodness. Amen.

What kind of God is God? What is He really like? If God were to come and be visible and physically present among us, how would we find Him to be? Granted, we can never come before His unapproachable light and expect our earthly intelligence to grasp it. But if we could, what kind of God would we find Him to be?

That question is one of the most important that any of us could ask, and our answer really defines who we are. In the history of the world, no nation has ever risen above its religion, and no religion has ever risen above its perception of God. Religion is high or low, base or pure, depending upon what the believers believe their God to be like. The history of Christianity will demonstrate that Christianity at any given time is weak or powerful, dependent upon what kind of God it perceives Him to be.

The local church is greater, smaller, powerful, or weak—and I am not talking about numbers, for there can be great small churches—depending upon what they think of God. The same goes for the individual Christian. If I could find out what you really perceive God to be like, I could prophesy your future without much trouble, for you are always going to move in the direction of your perception of God.

The most important thing for us to do is to constantly work on our perception of God.

One of the perceptions we have of God is that He is good, and that out of His goodness flows mercy. God is kindhearted and of goodwill. In other words, God is kindly and cordial, and we might even say good-natured with a benevolent intention. God is not kindhearted a little bit; He is infinitely kindhearted. He is not gracious and cordial a little bit or a great deal; He is perfectly and infinitely gracious and good. Whatever God is, He is completely and enthusiastically. God is not some absentee engineer running His universe by remote control. God is present in perpetual, continual eagerness, applying His holy designs with all the fervor of His rapturous love.

God, being who He is, cannot be indifferent. It is impossible for God to be indifferent. Either God loves with a boundless, unremitting energy, or God hates with a consuming fire. God said certain people were neither hot nor cold—that is, they were in between, half-asleep, lukewarm, so He would spew them out of His mouth. God cannot be halfway on a question; either He loves with an infinite, boundless, overwhelming, and enthusiastic energy of love, or He hates with an uncompromising fire of holy hatred.

In thinking about this, let me say that no one has any right to say that God has an obligation toward someone. God has no obligation toward anyone. He has no obligation to anything. When we think of the creation of the world, God, out of His own goodness, willed it into being. The good, enthusiastic, kindhearted God willed to create everybody and everything, and make the heavens and the earth, and hang the stars in their place. He willed to do it. He did it out of His own goodness. He did not owe anybody anything. He did not do it to perfect himself, because He was perfect to start with; and there was no start per se, because when we say that God started, then we make a creature out of Him.

God is uncreated, timeless, and contains time within His heart.

Let me ask you this: Why, when we sin, are we not destroyed? You can write as many books on the subject as you want, but I can give it to you in one sentence: Because God in His goodness willed to spare us, and that is the only answer. If you pay a man to lecture ten times, an hour each lecture, on why God spared humanity, he cannot tell you one thing more. God spared us and did not send us immediately to hell because He in His goodness willed to spare us.

Also, why did He suffer and die in agony when He did not need to do it? The answer is His goodness. He loved us, and by His mercy and goodness, He died for us.

Why does God answer prayer? Because of His goodness. Why does God forgive sin? Because of His goodness. It is because God is kindhearted and gracious and of benevolent intention with all the enthusiasm of an infinitely powerful God. That is why He hears us and forgives us.

To understand this means that you cannot go to God and argue your good points, because you do not have any. You cannot go to God and argue, "Oh God, please bless us—because of thugs and so," and think that God will listen to you. You cannot argue God into doing something that would be contrary to His nature. If we learn that God does everything out of goodness, without any price and without any obligation, we will find God very easy to approach and find Him very wondrously near. Out of His goodness, God has ordained means to help us, and all those means are because of His goodness.

If you are baptized, it is not the water that has done you any good. God, out of His goodness, has ordained that if you will be baptized, you will be obeying His Word, and He will bless you for your obedience. So it is with everything.

"O God," the psalmist says, "in Thy mercy, hear my prayer." It is an act of God's mercy to hear my prayer, even if it is the holiest prayer ever prayed. Nobody could reach God, except God in His goodness has willed us to be able to reach Him. I think we can save people a lot of work if they can only grasp this about God. I believe our praying would rise and become effective, if we would see that the only claim we have is something that we do not personally have at all. It is the goodness of God. And, of course, the goodness of God was made possible toward us through His atonement.

Jesus Christ is the kindest man who ever lived in the world, and God is the kindest God. Jesus was the God-Man. The love of God, the mind of God, the heart of God is kinder than you can imagine. If you were to concentrate on the word kind for one hundred years, you would not be able to truly grasp how kind God is. He is so high that the archangels veil their faces before Him, but He is so good-natured and kindly disposed that He would pat the head of a little child, forgive a harlot on the street, and be merciful to Israel, to the church, and to all of us. Everything comes out of the goodness and mercy of God.

Another important truth we need to grasp is that God is not revolted by our wretchedness. God has no regrets about anything He has made. God is not revolted because of anything that we are or have done. When God created everything, He pronounced it good. All the sin in the entire universe could never take away from God that which He has established and called good.

I have not always been a kind man. Sometimes I have been sharp-tongued toward people and may have offended people, but God is not like that at all. I could never have been a nurse because dirty things make me gag. God never gagged at anything He created and has never been revolted by the humblest thing. There is nothing in your body or in your soul that turns God away from you. God is never revolted by you or disgusted by you, no matter how sinful, how impure, or how odd you may be; He never turns away, because God is good.

Out of God's goodness flows His mercy. Again, let me state that mercy is an attribute of God; it is not something that God has—it is something God is. If mercy were something God had, He might use it up or leave it somewhere and forget it, but mercy is what God is. If anybody should ask what kind of God your God is, simply reply, "Our God is good." And should they say, "Tell me more," say, "Our God is merciful." He not only has mercy, but He is mercy. It is something God is, and it is as eternal as God.

God's goodness is a source of mercy, and God is of infinite goodness—that is, He desires His creatures' happiness. God desires that you be joyful. He will allow you to suffer if that suffering will make you holy, because He wants you to be holy. The trouble with this is we try to get happy right away, after suffering, whereas God wants us to be holy in order that our happiness might last. Unholy happiness cannot last; it can only spring up like a dandelion and perish tomorrow. So God takes us through many fires and many trials, and it is not so important that we be happy right now. He is thinking about our enjoyment forever. This is part of the goodness and mercy of God.

God has an irresistible urge to bless people. He wants to bless you and your family and your business and your church.

God takes pleasure in the pleasure of His people. He suffers along with His friends, and He takes no pleasure in the suffering of His enemies.

Some of the monks of old used to beat their backs with whips and sleep in beds of spikes, thinking they could coax God into being more merciful. There is nothing you can do to increase God's mercy. The mercy of God is as big as God, and God fills all space and overflows into a vacuity, so that you cannot add anything to His grace and mercy. Your coaxing cannot add anything to God's mercy. You do not have to go to God and build a case for yourself, or throw up your hands and say, "God, be merciful unto me!" God will have mercy on you because God is merciful. That is the way God is. That is the way we can expect Him to be all the time—not part of the time, but all of the time.

God is the same good and merciful God at all times, without any change. If God could become less than himself and be imperfect, He would be no God at all. To be God and remain God, He has to remain all that He is forever, and merciful is one thing that He is. You can be sure you will never find God in a bad mood. You will never find God saying, "I am not going to be nice today. I am not going to bless them."

Nothing that occurs or ever can occur can ever increase the mercy of God, diminish the mercy of God, or alter the quality of God's mercy. William Shakespeare wrote:

The quality of mercy is not strained.

It droppeth as the gentle rain from heaven

Upon the place beneath. It is twice blessed:

It blesseth him that gives and him that takes.

Some people believe that when Jesus came and was born in a manger and the angels sang, God became merciful. But it was the mercy of God that sent Jesus to Bethlehem's manger.

Someone else says, "When Jesus died on the cross, then God became merciful." No, a thousand times no. He died on the cross because God was already merciful, and nothing Jesus did when He came into the world made God any more merciful than He already was. It was the mercy of God and the goodness of God that brought Him, and when Jesus rose from the dead and ascended to the right hand of God, the Father Almighty, He did not become any more merciful. God had been kind and loving all the time.

The same God who is merciful is also just and holy, and holiness cannot possibly have any fellowship with unholiness. Justice, when it confronts human iniquity, demands judgment, but when mercy confronts human guilt and suffering, it wants to be merciful and can be, because Christ died. Christ came, died, rose, and lives in order that mercy might flow down like a fountain. The cross is God's channel. Jesus Christ's dying and rising is the way mercy flows. It is the direction mercy takes, so all the poor sinner needs to do is step into the framework of the cross and believe on His Son. Turn your back on iniquity, and you will find that the mercy of God will confront your guilt and suffering and pronounce you clean.

All of us are recipients of the mercy of God.

Mercy cannot cancel sin until there has been atonement for sin, but there has been atonement. Jesus Christ died, and what He did was absolutely complete. You do not have to know all about the atonement. You only have to know that Jesus Christ came down to die for you, and because of what He did, the mercy of God can flow to you like a river.

In dying, Jesus suffered a long time. I say again, I do not know how the perfect God could suffer. But I can bow my head and say, "Oh, Lord God, thou knowest."

Alas! and Did My Savior Bleed

Alas! and did my Savior bleed,

And did my Sovereign die!

Would he devote that sacred head

For sinners such as I?

Was it for crimes that I have done,

He groaned upon the tree?

Amazing pity! Grace unknown!

And love beyond degree!

Well might the sun in darkness hide,
And shut its glories in,
When God, the mighty maker, died
For his own creature's sin.

Thus might I hide my blushing face
While his dear cross appears;
Dissolve my heart in thankfulness,
And melt mine eyes to tears.

But drops of tears can ne'er repay
The debt of love I owe.
Here, Lord, I give myself away;
'Tis all that I can do.
Isaac Watts
(1674–1748)

Chapter 14

A High and Lofty Perception of God

Thine, O Lord, is the beauty, the glory, the victory, and the majesty. All that is in the heaven and earth is Thine. Thine is the kingdom, O Lord. Wherever I look, I see Thy fingerprints, and my heart sings forth Thy praise. Amen.

Although they do not mean to do it necessarily, theologians have a way of hiding truth behind big words and chasing people away. I have a little tip: You can understand anything any theologian can understand. Do not let them fool you.

The doctor may write his prescription in Latin, hit the layman on the head, and make him feel as if he is up against something big when he sees those Latin words, which he cannot even read. Theologians do the same thing. They talk about the divine transcendence and everybody runs out, buys a novel, and says, "I'll read what I can understand."

We can understand theology as presented to us in the Bible. We can understand what God says in the Bible about himself, although we may never plumb the depths of understanding it intellectually.

Take divine transcendence, for example. It means that God is above, high up and above all things. Supposedly, that contradicts His immanence, which means God is in every place and God is here. God's omnipresence will comfort you better than your own breath. It will comfort you in your soul. Your own thoughts are heard by Him just as loud as your loudest shout, because God is as near to you as your own breath, as near to you as your blood, as near to you as your nerves, as near to you as your thoughts and your soul.

God is so high up that He cannot even be conceived. I need to explain now what I mean by "so high up" or "far above." I do not mean distant, because God does not care anything about distance. God is not high up in the astronomical sense; He is not high up in the sense that He is a ray of light beyond Mars.

It is important that we think of God as being in His right character, so infinitely beyond everything that you and I know that we cannot explain it. Physical magnitude does not mean anything to God. Never suppose that God is at the top of the ascending curve of life. That is a great mistake. In some people's circle of life, they start with one creature and move their way up a little bit to the birds, and then they go all the way up to beasts and then all the way up to man. Then they think they are on their way up to the archangels and then the burning cherubim, and then at the top of that circle of life is God. That is no way to think of God at all.

Would you be shocked to know that God is just as high above archangels as He is above a caterpillar? The gap that separates the archangel from the caterpillar is of finite depth. How quickly we are to think that the angel has a grade of life that is far higher than the caterpillar that crawls in the room. They are alike in that they are creatures. There was a time that they were not, and then they were. The archangel with his broad wings spread and the tiny caterpillar inching its way along are both creatures of God.

But God is not a creature. He does not belong in the creature category. We must think of God as separated from, high above, way beyond, and other than. He is God, and there is nothing like God in the entire universe. Only God is God.

When we think of God as being high above, the substance of God is wholly above, and God can never pass over and cease to be God, and nothing that is not God can ever pass over and become God. The idea that Jesus was a man who became God is not true. Jesus was God and man united in one being. There was never such a thing as man becoming God, and there never can be such a thing as God becoming a creature. That would be to bring God down and falsify the majesty of deity.

This is the great God, the One you and I are called to serve. All of the things that are said or taught about God are only a portion of God and a small part of His ways. We have what is called the rational element, which is the part you can get hold of with your finite mind.

People would like to pull God down and make Him small so that they could have a God their size—though a little bigger, so He could help them when they are in trouble. That is the kind of God that is in evangelical circles today. The God of the average evangelical church is too small. He is not the God of the heavens and of creation, but He is a homemade, handmade God pulled down to our level. Our God today is like an old uncle whom we want to keep on good terms, and when the time comes, He will make us rich or help us in some way in a business deal. We want to be able to use God for our purposes.

Let me say clearly: I would not bow my knees to that kind of a God. The God that can get me on my knees has to be infinitely higher than I am. He must be so high and lofty and glorious that I could join the angels, seraphim, and cherubim to cry, "Holy, holy, holy, Lord God of Saboath." He would have to be so mighty that He could put the world in His hand, and He would have to be bigger than the devil, greater and mightier than mountains, and grander than fire. He would have to be all that and much more to be a God I could worship.

The God whom I could think up with my head, I will never get down on my knees to worship—never.

I am an American, and I do not bow to people easily. I do not like the idea of classes, where some men are big shots and some are little shots, and the little shots get down on their knees before the big shots. That is not the way it should be in America, and that is not the way to do it as a Christian.

God made us all so that the humblest little child is just as valuable to God as a Christian with lots of money to write big checks and drive big cars. Let us keep ourselves as free as we can. And remember, when it comes to God, we go down on our knees along with the mighty man and the potentate and the humble man. Let us not get big ideas about these important people and think that they are more important to God.

When we say, "I accept Jesus," we are not doing Jesus any favor. Some evangelists make it out as though you will be doing Jesus a great favor if you come to Him. No, you do not do Jesus any favor when you give your heart to Him. And He does not lose anything when you refuse to give your heart to Him. You hold off, and He loses nothing. Give, and He gains nothing. He already has the world without end. Multitudes of the redeemed and the four beasts at the altar and the living creatures all bow before Him and cry, "Holy, holy, holy, worthy is the Lamb that was slain."

Let us not imagine we are doing Jesus a favor by testifying or witnessing. We are not doing Jesus a favor by giving our hearts to Him. Rather, He is doing us an infinite favor by accepting us and receiving us unto himself. The mighty God looked at man, and took upon Him flesh as man, and died and rose again. Now we are set before this mighty Lord Jesus. So do not get too proud. It was Jesus who rose from the dead and said, "All power is given unto me in heaven and on earth," and He is not going to, for one second, allow himself to be pawed and slobbered over by carnal men and women whose concept of love came from Hollywood.

I understand that certain Muslims who cannot read, if they see a paper lying on the ground and do not know what is written on it, put it up carefully on a shelf somewhere, where it is safe. They are afraid that the sacred name of Allah might be written on it. They do not want to be guilty of trampling on that sacred name. They are more reverent than many Christians. They bow before Allah more than many Christians go before the Father, Son, and Holy Spirit.

The question is simple: Do you know this awesome God? This God the philosophers have called the mysterium tremendum—the tremendous mystery, the awesome mystery. Before this mysterium tremendum, Jacob cried, "How dreadful is this place; this is the house of God." In the New Testament, Peter said, "Depart from me, Lord, for I am unclean." Abraham said, "I am but dust and ashes."

Job was speechless before God. Job was an orator and probably would have made a good politician or an evangelist. He could open his mouth and words would flow out like water out of a flask. But when God revealed himself to him, Job laid his hands on his mouth and said, "O God, I cannot speak."

Many people are not getting anyplace with God because they have never met that kind of God. Their God is a self-made God and carries with Him no mystery or majesty. I will never bow my knee to a self-made or handmade God. I bow my knee to that mysterium tremendum—that awesome majesty we call our Father, which art in heaven.

I have been teaching and preaching since I was nineteen years old, and I must confess that the older I get, the dumber I get. I know so little. People come and ask me things that I could answer by pointing it out in the Bible. However, honesty compels me to confess that I do not know very much anymore. Once I knew a lot, or thought I did, but as I spend time before this tremendous God, I become more and more aware that I do not know very much anymore. And really, I believe it ought to work this way.

Nobody who is proud will ever be acceptable to the awesome presence of the most holy God. The God who knows all that can be known in one easy, effortless act, and knows all power, all spirits, all minds, all matter, all relationships, all energy, all history, and all the future—compared to this God, I know very little.

None of us knows very much, and the man who thinks he knows the most is the man who, according to Paul, knows the least. If we would just admit how utterly ignorant we are, we would begin to get somewhere with God.

God is not interested in your head. He is not interested in how many degrees you have. After I received my honorary degree, I did not preach any better, nor did I pray any better. Degrees do not mean anything, and yet some people imagine that if they do not have a degree, they cannot get anywhere. Some of the simplest people in the world know God far better than a person with a PhD does. Pray with your heart, and God will hear you.

Some people will come to the altar and pray and then go away disappointed. The reason is they have a controversy with God. They are holding out on God, fighting Him. Do not be fooled on this. God is still the awesome God that sent fire on the cities of Sodom and

Gomorrah and turned the people into ashes. He is still that God.

If you have a dispute with God, keep in mind two things: One, you cannot win, and two, God cannot lose. If you are fighting God at any point, you have no chance of winning. My advice is, simply, to quit your fighting, surrender, and say, "God, here I am." Throw yourself into the hands of God. You cannot win as long as you are resisting God, and God cannot lose because He is sovereign and is working according to a plan He established before the foundation of the world. When it is all over, the crown will be on the head of Jesus, and His bride will walk with Him into the presence of the Father, with great joy. God will win in the end.

All those who fight will lose. Either God will win over you now, to your everlasting blessedness, or God will win over you later, to your everlasting loss and sorrow and shame. Stop fighting God and you will win peacefully, for God loves you, and Jesus died for you, and the Holy Spirit is anxious to apply the blood and break every fetter in your life and set you free. He cannot do it, however, while you resist Him.

Noti, But Christ

Not I, but Christ, be honored, loved, exalted;

Not I, but Christ, be seen be known, be heard;

Not I, but Christ, in every look and action,

Not I, but Christ, in every thought and word.

Not I, but Christ, to gently soothe in sorrow;

Not I, but Christ, to wipe the falling tear;

Not I, but Christ, to lift the weary burden!

Not I, but Christ, to hush away all fear.

Not I, but Christ, in lowly, silent labor;

Not I, but Christ, in humble, earnest toil;

Christ, only Christ! no show, no ostentation!

Christ, none but Christ, the gath'rer of the spoil.

Christ, only Christ, ere long will fill my vision;

Glory excelling, soon, full soon, I'll see—

Christ, only Christ, my every wish fulfilling—

Christ, only Christ, my All in all to be.

A. B. Simpson

(1843–1919)

Chapter 15

The Effect of Our Perception of God

Our hearts sing in praise and adoration as we experience Thy presence, O God, in our day-to-day living. It would be one thing to worship Thee one day, but to be able to worship Thee every day, and all day long, is the great joy of knowing Thee. Amen.

Somebody asked Charles Spurgeon once if he ever preached a sermon more than once. "Do you think," he replied, "I would throw away the ax after I cut down the tree?" I know exactly how he felt, and I feel the same way. You run the risk of repeating yourself if you teach for very long. I am of the nature that if what I am saying is helpful, not only do I want to repeat it, but also I give everyone permission to repeat it without giving me any credit. After all, it is the message that really matters.

I think everybody ought to have the privilege of using any of the Lord's weapons belonging to the Lord's people, except their armor. Remember, Saul's armor did not fit David, and I will never wear anybody's armor except mine.

Let me outline a few things along this line of knowing God.

The first is that life is a serious thing, and this is a serious world in which we live.

I am encouraged that there are still among us enough serious-minded people who realize the seriousness of life and are honestly concerned about how they can meet and conquer life and death—about how they can salvage something out of the wreck of this world and how they can save their own souls out of a disaster. "Save yourselves," Peter cautioned, "from this untoward generation." If an apostle said this, I think I can whisper it today.

I think there are some who want to save their souls from this untoward generation—this coming crash and downfall of the world. In light of this, I would like to give them counsel, not from a perfect man, but from someone who has walked with God, who has loved and lived the Scriptures for quite a while, and who has no other motive except to do you good.

Nobody can get my ear or my respect if I know he has a hand extended. I do not think this is such a spiritual thing; I have no conscience about it at all. I plug my ears against the man who I suspect is just out to get something. However, no man can talk too strictly to me if I know he loves me and does not want anything I have. And no man can be too eloquent for me to walk out on if I have a suspicion that he wants something I have.

If we are going to save ourselves from this untoward generation and salvage something out of the world, I think four things need to be put in focus in our everyday lives.

The first is that our perception of God needs to be in line with the God of the Bible. In other words, we should be magnifying God in our daily lives.

I am positively sure after many years of observation and prayer, that the basis of all our trouble today in religious circles is that our God is too small, that our God is not big enough. This cannot be repeated too many times. I do not think we can make God big, because that is completely beyond our ability. We cannot have an imaginary God. We must see God as He has delighted to reveal himself, especially in the Word of God.

I believe that the most important verse in the Bible is—and this is a very hard thing to say because the Bible is such a magnificent book—"In the beginning God..."

This is the most important verse because that is where everything must begin. God is the fountain out of which everything springs, and He is the foundation upon which everything rests. God is all in all. I am quite sure that if we would begin to see our God bigger, we would also begin to see people smaller. This is the day of the magnification of slick personalities, and as we magnify slick personalities, we are, in fact, minimizing God. We have church meetings in which we never see God at all. We see only the servants of God, which is a tragedy.

I am afraid that we have a lot of hero worship in the church of Christ today. We are magnifying the messenger and consequently minimizing the message. The message should be of such a nature that it overshadows the messenger.

God moves according to an eternal purpose, and He carries on after His own plans. He does not need anybody to direct Him, correct Him, or qualify what He has to say. The most astounding and powerful phrase in all of Scripture is "Thus saith the Lord." After that, nothing more needs to be said. God is enough.

The creeds have taught us that God is a spirit, infinite, eternal, and unchangeable in His being, wisdom, power, holiness, justice, goodness, and truth. With the contemplation of God's majesty, all eloquence fades into the shadows. Man's eloquence cannot rise high enough to give praise worthy enough to this One we refer to as the mysterium tremendum.

Man's language can never be adequate enough to fully express the worthiness of our God. Many wordsmiths throughout the years have tried to honor God with language. Language can never fully express God in all His majestic wonderment. We try, and the hymn writers have done a great job of doing it, but even they fall short of the glory that belongs only to God.

Sometimes in our prayers, we get rather eloquent. I have discovered that when I am the most eloquent in my prayers, I am not getting very much accomplished. My eloquence sometimes gets in the way of really connecting with God.

I tell you, our feelings can never be boiled down to mere words. There is something about God that is so majestic and so awe-inspiring as to frustrate expression.

I have been an eager reader of Shakespeare, but even he lacks the ability to articulate the majesty of God in words and phrases that are worthy of God. No matter what we say, no matter how we say it, our God is bigger. When I try to express my love for God, words get in the way, and sometimes I am even brought to a place of silence. It is in the silence that my appreciation of God raises itself in a worthy manner.

If I had the talent and ability of Shakespeare, of Francis Bacon, of Henry Thoreau, of John Milton—the list could go on and on—I could never adequately express to God what is worthy of Him. To know God in the fullness of His revelation is to feel a deep sense of inadequacy in our worship. Those who are happy with their worship have probably never been in the presence of God. When I am on my face before God in worship, there is such a feeling of inadequacy as I come before this holy One. How can I come as imperfect and limited as I am and bring to the holy, unlimited One that which is worthy of Him?

Why is this? Why is it that I have difficulty expressing in my worship what is worthy and acceptable to God?

The basic reason is the flesh. God cannot accept anything of the flesh. No matter where you go in the Scriptures, you will find that the flesh is always contrary to God's will. The flesh needs to be dealt with in our everyday lives. Nothing of the flesh is pleasing unto God.

The greatest expression of the flesh is entertainment. The world has honed this to absolute perfection. Entertainment has taken over in our culture today, and nothing can be done apart from it. The error that we make is this: We think we can entertain God. We believe that what we do and how we do it will bring a sense of pleasure to God.

What we need to understand is that God cannot be entertained, especially by the flesh. Once we get this into our heads, we begin to look at our relationship with God a little differently. God is not going to entertain me, and God is not going to be entertained by me. This fact rules out a lot that passes for worship today.

Entertainment is simply the demonstration of the flesh at its finest moment. Because this is acceptable in the world, many think it is acceptable to God. Most of our church worship services are simply religious entertainment. If it is entertainment, it is really not of God. Worship and entertainment are not synonymous, yet many in our evangelical churches today think they are. Sunday morning to some has become a time of religious musical entertainment, thinking that it is pleasing unto God.

The God of the Bible is of such a nature that He is worthy of that which is compatible with His nature. Entertainment is not compatible with the nature of God. If we are going to please God, we need to please Him on His terms. If we are going to worship God, we must worship Him on His terms.

Dealing with the flesh in the church today is probably the most difficult thing that we will ever do. If we can deal with the flesh elements in the church, we will release congregations to positions of worship acceptable unto God.

Although I am not dealing with the gifts of the Spirit in this book, I simply would point out that God can be served and worshiped only through the gifts of the Spirit. Man's talent falls far short of that which is pleasing unto God. The flesh cannot do the work of the ministry or the worship of God. Somehow we have lost this concept.

What are some people going to do if they get to heaven and find out there is not one bit of entertainment throughout all the golden streets? The golden streets are certainly not Broadway. Heaven is not a place of entertainment. Heaven is a place of worship, and the object of the worship is God. The more I know about God, the more I will begin to understand what kind of worship is acceptable and what is not acceptable. This is why it is important for me to have a clear, precise perception of God as He truly is.

Once I understand God and the worship and the ministry that are acceptable to Him, I need to move on into one area, which is to magnify God in everything I do. Again, let me point out, the flesh cannot magnify God. I need to deal with the flesh so that I can magnify God in every aspect of life. If there is one aspect of my life where God is not magnified, there is no aspect of my life where He is worthily magnified.

Dealing with the flesh is a very serious matter because it brings me to the point of worthily magnifying God. What does it mean to magnify God?

To put it bluntly, it simply means to make God big in your life. The more you get to know God and understand His holiness, the more you will begin to magnify God in your life, and then God will become the biggest thing in your life. If something in your life is bigger than God, I can assure you that God is not in your life. The goal that I have as a Christian is to magnify God. The great discipline of the Christian life is to live in a way that magnifies God.

The word that is used in this regard is to mortify the flesh. That is simply to turn your back on the flesh and reckon your flesh to be dead. "I am crucified with Christ," Paul said, "nevertheless I live; yet not I, but Christ liveth in me: and the life which I now live in the flesh I live by the faith of the Son of God, who loved me, and gave himself for me" (Galatians 2:20).

This is to put a death sentence on everything about my life. I cannot be one way on Sunday morning and different come Monday morning. I cannot be one way when I am around Christians and completely different when around other people. Some claim to have mortified the flesh, but they still have the spirit of resentfulness, they still love money, and they still have a temper. Either mortify the flesh or the flesh will destroy you and your Christian testimony.

I must confess some of the most delightful meetings that I have been in have been where God is present in such awesome power that the people were afraid to move. At times, the presence of God was so thick on the assembly that nobody could even whisper. God was indeed in that place.

If more of our churches would experience this on a regular basis, the trend for entertainment would quickly disappear. There is no entertainment anywhere or by anyone that can compare with the manifest presence of God upon an assembly of believers. As we mature in the Lord, we lose our desire for the toys of religion. They no longer satisfy, and the only thing that really satisfies is God's presence in our midst. It is not about a good show. It is not about being entertained and enthusiastically lifted up. If I can be lifted up enthusiastically, I can come crashing down too. But when I am in the presence of God and He manifests himself to me, there is nothing artificial. I can never get over that experience, the experience of practicing the presence of God. Again, let me say, we must deal with the flesh.

I have been accused many times of being radical, and I do not mind that at all. I think you have got to be a little bit radical if you are going to follow the Lord Jesus Christ, so I am not afraid of being radical. If you really want to see an increased experience in the presence of God, let me offer a few suggestions.

Go home and begin pulling the plug on all those things in your home that are simply there for entertainment. I am talking about your radio, your TV, and maybe even your telephone. I know we need the telephone for a lot of reasons, but there are times that we need to cut ourselves off so completely from the world that all we have left is God. That is all right with me. I want to be in such a situation that all I have is God.

You do not need to know so much, and you do not need to have so many things. If your life is down to the basics, it will enable you to hold on to the faith once delivered to the saints, for as Brother Lawrence has said, "Practice the presence of God."

One last thought along this line would be to cultivate a servant attitude.

David, after he had served his own generation by the will of God, fell asleep. I firmly believe that no man has any right to die until he has served his generation. As a Christian, when I die, I want to make sure that the world around me is in debt to me because of my service.

When John and Charles Wesley came into the world, they were in debt to their mother, to their father, to their nurse, and to everyone who served them. They did not die until they turned the tables on the world, and now the world and the church of God are in debt to John and Charles Wesley. It is hardly possible to have a church service without singing one of Charles Wesley's hymns.

Down the line we could go in the great Hall of Faith. One by one we could see those who have come into the world owing everybody everything, and then when they died, they reversed the tables, and now the whole world is indebted to them. Why? Because they had a servant mentality. This is crucial, and it flows from a proper perception of who God is.

You cannot serve the last generation, because it is gone. In addition, you can only indirectly serve the next generation, but you can serve this present generation. Too many Christians are simply religious sponges; they absorb and absorb and absorb, and that is about all there is to their lives. However, the Lord wants us to serve, to do things for people, to put people in debt to us. As we magnify God, crucify the old man, simplify our lives, and cultivate a servant attitude, we put this generation and generations to come in debt to us.

Revive Thy Work, O Lord

Revive Thy work, O Lord,

Thy mighty arm make bare;

Speak with the voice that wakes the dead,

And make Thy people hear.

Revive Thy work, O Lord,

Disturb this sleep of death;

Quicken the smoldering embers now

By Thine almighty breath.

Revive Thy work, O Lord,

Create soul-thirst for Thee;

And hungering for the bread of life

O may our spirits be.

Revive Thy work, O Lord,
Exalt Thy precious name;
And, by the Holy Ghost, our love
For Thee and Thine inflame.

Revive Thy work, O Lord,
Give Pentecostal showers;
The glory shall be all Thine own,
The blessing, Lord, be ours.
Albert Midlane
(1825–1909)

Chapter 16

Our Perception of God Navigates Our Prayer Life

O God, my greatest joy is the joy I find in that secret fellowship with Thee. Nothing else fills my heart with such excitement and enthusiasm as coming into Thy presence, knowing that I am welcome. May my life today be saturated with prayer and praise because of who I know Thee to be. Amen.

In my mind, the most important discipline in my life has to be my prayer life. It is one thing to talk about prayer. No matter where you go, Christians celebrate the virtues of prayer and a prayer life. Yet I find it rather strange, when you get down to the practical aspects, very few Christians really engage in the discipline of prayer to the extent that is available to them in their Christian experience.

It was George Mueller who observed that he had so much to do that he could not afford to spend less than four hours a day in prayer. There was a man who understood the place of prayer. We would say that we have so much to do we cannot afford to spend time in prayer. Compare our lives with the life of George Mueller, and see who really had the best idea of prayer.

When Jesus died on the cross, rose the third day from the grave, ascended into heaven, and was seated at the right hand of God the Father, He established for us an access to the very ear of God. I am not sure if Christians realize the dynamics of this access. We now have access to the ear of the God and Father of our Lord Jesus Christ. It is a humbling concept to process as I ponder and meditate on my relationship with God.

My relationship to God is not arbitrary, nor is it ritualistic. Rather, it is a personal experience, and it is more than a monologue—it is a dialogue. I am afraid most Christians have not progressed to the dialogue aspect of their prayer life.

Our perception of God is what really establishes the perimeters, if you please, of our prayer life. We need to understand that prayer is not a meritorious act. We do not earn anything because of it. We pray because God hears, and God hears us because of Jesus. Because of Him, God the Father has a good heart toward His people.

The pagans pray to sticks and stones and all sorts of man-made things, without any merit in their prayers whatsoever. The impressive thing, and the most disappointing, is their utter commitment and discipline to this bogus prayer life. God hears us not because our prayer is good, but because God is good. One dear brother used to cup his ear and say, "God stoops and cups His ear to hear me pray." The dear brother was not far from the truth. Prayer is the means that God has of knowing that we are ready to receive what He wants us to have.

My perception of the goodness of God will guide me in my prayer. I need to understand that I do not have to talk God into doing something that He may not want to do. Listen to some of the prayers at a prayer meeting, and you would think people believe they can talk God into something He does not want to do. This is absolutely not true.

God cannot be talked into doing something He does not want to do or that is against His character and nature and attributes. I cannot convince God to do something because I want Him to do it. I am not in the position, nor is anyone else, to negotiate with God on my terms.

The more I begin to understand the goodness of God, the more I begin to understand my relationship to Him, and the more I begin to understand what prayer is all about. God's goodness is the ground of our expectation when it comes to prayer. What can we really expect God to do?

The more I get to know what kind of God is, the more I will begin to understand what my expectation from Him is and what His expectation of me is. It goes both ways, you know. Most confusion in my prayer comes from my not fully understanding what God's expectation of me is. Remember, prayer is not trying to conform God to our situation, but rather our conforming to Him.

When I go to God, confess my sins, and trust Him to forgive me, by faith I accept His forgiveness. I am expecting God to forgive me, because I know that God is good and desires to forgive me because of Jesus' sacrifice for me. Does the merit lie in my faith? Never. It lies in the good God who forgives because He is gracious, kind, and ready to forgive.

So many Bible verses blossom and flower when we think of the goodness of God.

The goodness of God leads us to repentance, Paul says in Romans: "Or despisest thou the riches of his goodness and forbearance and longsuffering; not knowing that the goodness of God leadeth thee to repentance?" (Romans 2:4).

David said in the Psalms, "Surely goodness and mercy shall follow me all the days of my life: and I will dwell in the house of the LORD forever" (Psalm 23:6).

As I begin to understand the goodness of God, I understand that He takes no pleasure in judgment. He does not take pleasure in the death of the wicked. God does judge, though. I believe in the judgment day and that every man shall receive according to his deeds done in the body. I believe there shall be a resurrection of the just and the unjust, and there shall be a resurrection of man unto eternal life and of man unto damnation. I believe that. Yet God takes no pleasure in judgment. David says that the Lord will rejoice over thee for good. God is delighted to shower our lives with His goodness.

When I was a young boy, I used to hear a little song:

In the Shadow of His Wings

In the shadow of His wings

There is rest, sweet rest;

There is rest from care and labor,

There is rest for friend and neighbor;

In the shadow of His wings

There is rest, sweet rest,

In the shadow of His wings

There is rest (sweet rest).

Jonathan B. Atchinson

(1840–1882)

If only we could realize that God is that kind of God, we would never have a hangdog look and feeling in our heart. We would never need to go away with a deep sense of inferiority. There is quite a difference between real repentance and a feeling of inferiority that makes you feel "I am no good. There is no use to pray; I am just no good."

Of course, you are no good. God is good, and because He is good, we can dare to take advantage of His goodness. God's door is always open for any of His children who have done wrong, so they can come to the point of saying, "Oh taste and see that the Lord is good."

Recently, as I spent a little time with the Lord each day, I was overwhelmed with how kind God has been to me. How utterly good He has been. If it were not for the grace of God, I would be roasting in hell or languishing in jail somewhere. God's goodness has surrounded me and pardoned me and forgiven me, and His loving-kindness has made my life reasonably decent, only because He is good, not because I am good.

I have a little book I have never been without for years. It is a little prayer book, which I wrote myself. I guess it is maybe seventeen or eighteen years old, and I carry it around wherever I go. I write my prayers, and I have a little understanding with God. Because I, by nature and conduct, have been the worst man that ever lived, I want God to do more for me than for any man that ever lived. I have a right to ask that because where sin abounds, grace doth much more abound. And if the goodness of God specializes in hard cases, and if the goodness of God can shine brighter against the dark sky, I will provide the dark sky. Shine on, O goodness of God.

When I was a young man, I used to ride the railroads—that is, I used to sneak on board and ride them for free. When I was converted, God began to convict me of that, and I wanted to make up for riding the train all those years without paying. I had been riding around at the expense of the railroad company, and I owed them something. So I wrote to the traffic manager and said:

Dear Sir,

I have been converted to Jesus Christ and I am a Christian now, and I want to straighten out my life. A little while back, I rode from here to there, from there to here, without paying, and I would like you to send me the bill. I want to pay up.

Not long after, I got a return letter on one of the official B & O pieces of stationary. I opened the letter and read:

Dear Sir,

Your letter has been received. We note that you have been converted and want to live a Christian life, and we want to compliment you on this new act. We compliment you on becoming a Christian. Now, about what you owe us. We rather suppose you did not get very good service on our line when you traveled, and therefore we will just forget the whole thing.

Sincerely yours,

Traffic manager

I kept that letter for a long time. My conscience was clean and free. God was good to me. I could not pay the bill; I did not have enough money.

May I encourage you that God is a just and holy and good God. I know God is severe with unbelief and sin, but God is good, infinitely good, always good. And if you need Him, God will always be there for you.

Sweet Hour of Prayer

Sweet hour of prayer! Sweet hour of prayer!

That calls me from a world of care,

And bids me at my Father's throne

Make all my wants and wishes known.

In seasons of distress and grief,

My soul has often found relief,

And oft escaped the tempter's snare,

By thy return, sweet hour of prayer!

Sweet hour of prayer! Sweet hour of prayer!

The joys I feel, the bliss I share,

Of those whose anxious spirits burn

With strong desires for thy return!

With such I hasten to the place

Where God my Savior shows His face,

And gladly take my station there,

And wait for thee, sweet hour of prayer!

Sweet hour of prayer! Sweet hour of prayer!
Thy wings shall my petition bear
To Him whose truth and faithfulness
Engage the waiting soul to bless.
And since He bids me seek His face,
Believe His Word and trust His grace,
I'll cast on Him my every care,
And wait for thee, sweet hour of prayer!

Sweet hour of prayer! Sweet hour of prayer!
May I thy consolation share,
Still, from Mount Pisgah's lofty height,
I view my home and take my flight.
This robe of flesh I'll drop, and rise
To seize the everlasting prize,
And shout, while passing through the air,
"Farewell, farewell, sweet hour of prayer!"
William W. Walford
(1772–1850)

Chapter 17
Our Perception of God in Creation

All of creation, O Lord, sings of Thy praise. I look to the hills and think of Thee. The mountains show Thy majesty and strength. From the rivers, I see the flowing grace and goodness of Thy very nature. All creation joins in praise unto Thee, and so do I. Amen.

God's fingerprints are all over creation. The more we delve into the mystery of creation, the more we begin to see God's fingerprints. Not all scientific discoveries can eliminate it; they only strongly suggest that behind everything is a creator. To disavow a creator is to compromise intelligence. Nothing has appeared without something or someone behind it.

Who is this creator behind everything? is the question that really needs to be answered. This creator is the God who created all things, and He created everything with a purpose. Nothing throughout all creation is meaningless or purposeless. I will never be able to understand the purpose until I understand who is behind all of this.

Unfortunately, we have left nature and creation to the scientists who are trying to unravel the mystery of our universe. It is my opinion that nature should automatically lead us to God, who is described for us in the Word of God as the Creator. If you have nature without the Word of God, you have a mysterious somebody, but no personal connection.

I do not approach this as a scientist, but as one who is deeply in praise and worship of the creator. Everything in creation sings the praises of this mysterious creator. I cannot explain creation, but I can see through creation the marvelous fingerprints of a God who is magnificent, awesome, and wonderful.

It is in the universities where they blame Christians for what they call anthropomorphism. That is a long word, and some readers might not know what it means. Anthropos is a Greek word meaning "a man," so anthropomorphism means that we have made God in our image, in the image of a man. All we do is take the best qualities in a man and project them upward, and then we have God. If we see a kind man, we say, "All right, then God must be kind," and we project that kindness out of the heart of man up to God and say, "God is kind, and He is infinitely kind," and then we preach and teach about it.

When critics say our concept of the heavenly Father is only a manufactured one, they say, in effect, "I know that God isn't the way you say He is." To answer that, ask, "All right, how did you find that out? You can only find it out by either discovery or revelation. When did you discover God so that you can tell us what kind of God He is, and if you did not discover Him, then you had a revelation. Will you please tell us where the revelation came from? What is the revelation?"

It presumes that the critic knows something about God that we do not know, the Bible doesn't know, the prophets and apostles did not know, Jesus our Lord did not know, and church fathers and martyrs and reformers did not know.

People might also call you an anthropomorphic obscurantist, meaning you cover things up and keep them obscure. We do not believe that. We believe sinners cover things up and keep them obscure, and that the children of God do all things in the light. The obscurantist is the one right now who is sitting somewhere drawing up a dirty contract, a crooked contract to cheat a widow out of her property. There is your obscure fellow. He is hiding in the darkness, but the children of the light come into the light.

When I say God is love, they say, "That's what you would like to have God be like, and because you like to see love in people, you like to see love in God." The whole thing is nonsense to me. If God made man in His image, is it not reasonable to believe that the best things in a man would be the nearest to what God is? If you would like to see a mother showing tenderness over her baby, then where do you suppose she got that tenderness?

That love we have for each other, where did we get it? That pity we show for one another, where did we get it?

We got it all where we got our life. We got it from God, and though we are fallen and lost, this decency came from the heart of God.

"If ye then, being evil, know how to give good gifts unto your children, how much more shall your Father which is in heaven give good things to them that ask him?" (Matthew 7:11).

So instead of our running and hiding and admitting we are ignorant, we stand right up to these critics and name-callers and say, "Keep your long names. I believe in God and I believe God made me in His image, and I believe that every good there is in humanity came from God."

God is not the goodness that humanity has projected upward. Man was made in the image of God, and any decency that may be left in our fallen nature came from the heart of God.

God is kind, and this is taught or implied throughout the entire Scriptures.

You studied the multiplication tables—$2 \times 2 = 4$, $2 \times 3 = 6$, and $2 \times 4 = 8$, and so on—those are data, mathematical facts. They will remain the same for the rest of your life. Right on up through to the highest possible reaches of mathematics, it will still be true that $2 \times 2 = 4$. Then there is this datum of truth: God is good. You can go out into the world and see accidents, polio, murders, and all the rest, and when it is all finished, it does not change the fact that God is good. You can go down where men cheat each other and lie and misuse figures for their purposes and make $2 \times 2 = 7$ so they can fill their own pocketbook, but that does not change the fact that $2 \times 2 = 4$.

Therefore, you can see everywhere among men that they are fallen in evil ways. You can see cruelty and darkness, but it does not change the fact that God is good. That is the datum of truth. It is a foundation stone of all our belief about God.

It is necessary to human sanity to believe that God is good—that the God who is in the heavens above is not a malicious God or an unkind God or a God who promotes evil, but a God who promotes good. To allow God to be any other kind of God would be to upset and completely change our moral standard for mankind. It would mean to turn heaven into a hell and hell into a heaven. It would mean that good could be bad and bad could be good, and God could be the devil and the devil could be God.

Many times we try to rest our faith on texts and promises. True faith can rest only on the character of God. I believe, and I have faith, because I believe in the One in whom my faith is placed. I believe in a God who is good, and I never worry that God, behind my back, will mistreat me. I never need to worry for fear God will catch me when my back is turned and do something malicious, for there is no malice in the heart of God, only love. There is only goodness in the heart of God; that is all. Therefore, I need not worry.

Oh, what a contrast between the Christ who walked among men and the evil men among whom He walked—the malicious, beard-pulling, whispering men and the calm, quiet, loving Jesus with a tender look on His face for every harlot at His feet, every babe on the lawn, every sick child, and every pain and sorrow in the world. He walked among men with goodwill, and the men among whom He walked accused Him for His goodness and wished He were dead.

When they nailed him on a tree, they did not change His goodness. He did not turn on them and curse them. He said, "Father, forgive them, for they know not what they do." They could kill Him, but they could not destroy the goodness in His heart, His goodwill toward men.

I would like to point out something you may have overlooked. It is that God's goodness is the grounds of our expectation. We evangelicals have gone overboard and thrown out some very wonderful treasures. Our Puritan fathers and the old Presbyterians and Congregationalists and Baptists and Methodists used to preach about what they called natural theology, and they did not hesitate. They were not liberals or modernists; they were the church fathers and taught what they called natural theology. They said that God revealed himself in nature and that there was a theology that could be built just by looking around you. We all know that is true, but we are afraid to say that today; we are scared stiff. We are afraid somebody will come along and beat us over the head with a Scofield Bible and say, "Now, wait a minute here—you're a liberal." No, no, my brother, I am no liberal. I hope I am liberal, but I am not liberal in theology, and I am not a modernist. But I believe that God has, through His creation, declared certain things to be true of himself. I know the Psalms say so, and the prophets say so, and Paul says so. When I go along with an apostle of the New Testament, a prophet of the Old Testament, a psalmist of both testaments, I feel that I am in pretty good company, and I am not too badly frightened.

I take great comfort in the fact that this is my Father's world. When sin came into the world, it brought into creation an element contrary to the character and nature of God. The apostle Paul put it this way, "For we know that the whole creation groaneth and travaileth in pain together until now" (Romans 8:22). Even nature is suffering because of the sin of man.

What this world of ours will be like when sin has been finally and eternally removed from all creation is something we can hardly think of. Let them think of us as they will, and let them call us what they will. Our hope is in the fact that this is our Father's world, and He has this world's best interest in mind that will stand throughout all eternity.

This is My Father's World

This is my Father's world,

And to my listening ears;

All nature sings and round me rings

The music of the spheres.

This is my Father's world:
I rest me in the thought
Of rocks and trees, of skies and seas;
His hand the wonders wrought.

This is my Father's world,
The birds their carols raise,
The morning light, the lily white,
Declare their Maker's praise.
This is my Father's world,
He shines in all that's fair;
In the rustling grass I hear Him pass;
He speaks to me everywhere.

This is my Father's world,
O let me ne'er forget
That though the wrong seems oft so strong,
God is the Ruler yet.
This is my Father's world,
The battle is not done.
Jesus, who died, shall be satisfied,
And earth and heav'n be one.
Maltbie D. Babcock
(1858–1901)

Chapter 18

The Perception of Our Fullness in Jesus Christ

O Lord Jesus Christ, Thou who are the Living Word, I invite Thee to live in my heart and flow from me into the world around me. Let me deal with those issues in my life that would hinder Thee from doing all that Thou wouldst do in and through me. Amen.

Everybody talks about the Bible, and yet I wonder sometimes how much of the Bible they really believe in. From my experience with the Scriptures, there are only two ways to deal with them.

One way to deal with Scripture is to pull it down and understand it in the light of our personal experience. The other way is to rise up into Scripture and understand it in the light of its own intention and its own purpose.

Mostly, we reach up and pull the Word of God down until it is familiar, until it is on our level, and we do not get under much conviction.

Paul's prayer for the Ephesians is usually read by God's children in the light of their limited attainment:

For this cause I bow my knees unto the Father of our Lord Jesus Christ, of whom the whole family in heaven and earth is named, that he would grant you, according to the riches of his glory, to be strengthened with might by his Spirit in the inner man; that Christ may dwell in your hearts by faith; that ye, being rooted and grounded in love, may be able to comprehend with all saints what is the breadth, and length, and depth, and height; and to know the love of Christ, which passeth knowledge, that ye might be filled with all the fullness of God.

Ephesians 3:14–19

Lovely prayer, but it is usually looked upon as a misty, unattainable ideal that nobody can hope to reach in this life. It is something you shoot for—a dream, a hope, a perfection—that eludes you. It is like climbing a mountain that gets higher and higher as you go up.

I fear this is the trouble with most Christians today. We have developed what I call a psychology of ignoble contentment. We want to be comforted when we ought to be stirred up and made discontented. A noble discontent is always more desirable for a Christian than an ignoble contentment.

Too many these days are going about the country making contented Christians. This is one of the worst possible things that could be done in the church—make a Christian content. We should not want contentment, but a thirst and hunger after God. As long as we are without the thirst and hunger, we will be content. For a man who is neither hungry nor thirsty does not go to a restaurant or step up to a water fountain. It is only when he is hungry or thirsty that he looks for a way to satisfy himself.

There must be a better place for most of us Christians than we have found up till now.

Every time this is said, somebody rushes out from behind a bush or crawls out of the woodwork somewhere and says that he or she is what we are talking about. Every time I write an editorial to the effect that the church needs prophets, somebody will write and say, "You're right, and I am the man." When you talk or write about the deeper life and say to God's people they ought to be more spiritual than they are, somebody comes rushing out all aglow and says, "That's right, and I've got it."

If you follow those people around, you will find as a rule that they do not have what they think they have. I have not seen very many people that have anything I want in the area of spirituality.

I do not want to judge people, but just look at modern fundamentalism and evangelicalism and ask this question: Is this what Jesus Christ was talking about when He told us what was going to take place after He went into heaven? I do not think so. If what I see all around me these days is what Jesus described, then He was guilty of greatly overselling His product. He was guilty of great exaggeration, because have you noticed here that the Lord Jesus Christ raised expectation by description?

For instance, in John 4:14, Jesus said, "Whosoever drinketh of the water that I shall give him shall never thirst." And in John 6:35, He said, "I am the bread of life: he that cometh to me shall never hunger." In John 7:38, Jesus said, "He that believeth on me, as the scripture hath said, out of his belly shall flow rivers of living water." In John 14:26, He said that the "Comforter, which is the Holy Ghost, whom the Father will send in my name, he shall teach you all things." In John 15:26, He said this Comforter "whom I will send unto you from the Father, even the Spirit of truth, which proceedeth from the Father, he shall testify of me," and in John 16:8, "He will reprove the world of sin, and of righteousness, and of judgment." In John 17:24, He said "that they may behold my glory, which thou hast given me: for thou lovedst me before the foundation of the world."

Are these things reality among Christians today?

When we come to the epistles, they are constantly describing something that is of a different flavor from what we find around us today in even the best of evangelical circles. Read the New Testament without prejudice, with an open mind, and catch the flavor, catch the spiritual fragrance, and then sniff around where you go to church and the people you associate with and see if it smells the same. There is a synthetic something about modern Christianity, and it is not the same as what we see described here.

The Corinthians were about the least spiritual of the people to whom the apostle wrote, yet if they were to come into the average church today, they would set things on fire because they were a gifted people. They were a people that would fall on their faces and say, "God is in this place." They had something; they had a supernatural something. There was some carnality hanging around that Paul tried to get out, but there was also a lot of spirituality there, and to compare even the Corinthian church with our average church today would be ridiculous, just plain ridiculous, because we just do not have what they had. We just are not where they were. We are far beneath them. We have pulled the New Testament down, and all those high promises and expectations have been dragged down to the level of our mediocrity.

The man of God admonished, "Let us go on unto perfection." I would like to say that there is a better place spiritually than you now possess. There may be a rare few who have climbed the mountains and from those delectable mountains have seen the city of God. It may be that you are about to step over the river and enter into it. It may be, but most of the Lord's people these days are not quite there yet. There is a better place for you, and I want to direct you to that better place. To do so, I want to make you just as dissatisfied as I possibly can, because it is the only hope for any of us.

There is a better place for us, and we do not have to alter our doctrine to get there. You can be a spiritual, godly, Christ like, worshipful person and never change your doctrine at all. We have all the doctrine we need. We do not need to import anybody to teach us any new doctrine. It is not something new I need to learn. It is something new I need to experience, and what I experience lies within the framework of the simple gospel as we know it. We got the tree, all right. The trouble is, the tree is not blooming. Fundamentalism and evangelicalism are a tree in winter. It is not dead, because there is life in it, all right, but it is not flowering. God never meant the tree of correct doctrine to stand stark and cold with the wind whistling through its bare branches. He meant the tree of correct doctrine to blossom, flower, and bear fruit.

We do not have to hunt up some Greek teacher and get the marginal annotations from another translation, or have someone come from a foreign country to tell us all of this. All we have to do is get down on our knees with our New Testament and pray through that boundary. The ladder that stood up on the earth with its top reaching half way up is still there, and we do not need anything else, just our knees and a New Testament.

What is our trouble today?

Our trouble is, we hear sermon after sermon and do not get anywhere. Why do we push and push the old cart up the hill, and then slip and have to go back down and get it the next Sunday morning, and push it up again? The average church consists of fifty-two futile efforts that go on per year, plus perhaps two or three thrown in that we call "revival efforts." I think we should call them revival efforts rather than revivals. In some parts of the country, they call them protracted meetings. I think that perhaps is more honest. But we always slip back to where we were before. Spiritually, we hop up on Sunday, but then slip back on Monday. Then we come, repeat it Wednesday night maybe, and do the same thing on Sunday. In light of the soon coming of the Lord, it is a terrible thing; in light of the fact that some of us have not got too long yet to go, it is a terrible thing.

Why is this happening? This is happening because we have a lack of desire. We have not the desire we ought to have, and God's people are not hungry and thirsty anymore. Occasionally I run into somebody who is so hungry and thirsty that he is practically in agony. I do not worry too much about him, because I know he will get somewhere.

Why is there so much light now among God's people, yet so little delight? The Lord's children do not have much joy in God anymore. We have to whip it up, which is why we have song leaders who are as smooth as a willow in the wind and could dance anytime they want to and know just how to whip us up and finally get us going. Why is it that we have no delight in God and have to get it somewhere? I will tell you what I would rather do. I would rather hear a half-hour concert of folk music than to be in a so-called Christian meeting, where they have to whip me up all the time, and wave their arms and grin and show all thirty-two teeth in order to get me going.

We just do not have the delight that the Scriptures promise us. We have replaced the light with what we call methodology. A group of men will sit around and have what they call a panel discussion.

It used to be the worship service would burst forth, and everybody's delight brought other people in, and they got convicted before God because of the sheer delight of the spiritual life around them.

Now it is methodology. We are teaching methods. The panel discussion is made up of twelve people who do not know what they are talking about, who are sitting around pooling their ignorance. That is the way we get on now. There is much light, but not much delight. We have a great deal of truth, but it is not blossoming.

We need to see great saints once again in our fellowship. The greater the saint and the holier the man, the less likely he is to admit that he amounts to anything. However, in those saints of the past, they did have a treasure, they did see visions of God, they did have heaven open up to them, and they did have great freedom and great peace and great joy and great delight and great intimacy with God. They may not have had it every day, but they did have those experiences, and God had it written in the great "Hall of Faith" in Hebrews 11.

Some people just get old and become spiritually mediocre. They have been a Christian for years and have served in the church, but they still have spirituality that is mediocre at best. We used to ask a very pertinent question: "Are you as spiritual as you were last week?" Nobody does that now. Everybody takes for granted their spiritual situation, which in my opinion is not a good thing to do. We need to inquire, "How's your soul this Sunday morning, brother?" Rather, we say, "Who won the game last night?" As you look at the saints of old, you might want to ask, what made these saints the kind of saints that they were? It was the intensity of their desire after God. They wanted God more than they wanted anything else. They wanted God more than they wanted ease, comfort, fame, wealth, friends, or even life itself. They wanted God, the triune God, so their hearts panted after God as the deer pants after the water brooks.

Jesus Demands this Heart of Mine

Jesus demands this heart of mine—

Demands my wish, my joy, my care;

But, ah! How dead to things divine,

How cold, my best affections are!

'Tis sin, alas! With dreadful power,

Divides my Savior from my sight;

Oh, for one happy, shining hour

Of sacred freedom, sweet delight!

Oh let Thy love shine forth and raise

My captive powers from sin and death,

And fill my heart and life with praise,

And tune my last expiring breath.

Anne Steele

(1717–1778)